Signed English for the Classroom

Text by KAREN LUCZAK SAULNIER
Introduction by HARRY BORNSTEIN

Prepared under the supervision of the
staff of the Signed English Project

LILLIAN B. HAMILTON
HOWARD L. ROY, Consultant
HARRY BORNSTEIN, Director

Illustrated by RALPH R. MILLER, SR.

Kendall Green Publications
Gallaudet University Press
Washington, DC

Kendall Green Publications
An imprint of Gallaudet University Press
Washington, DC 20002
http://gupress.gallaudet.edu

ISBN 0-913580-37-6

Table of Contents

Page

TO TEACHERS

We believe that your efforts to teach your students language will be more successful if you provide them with clear, unambiguous linguistic input. By signing and saying all that you feel is meaningful to your students, they will, in a most natural way, internalize this language and later use it in a spontaneous and appropriate manner. Consistent exposure to clear and complete language patterns should eliminate the need for much of the classroom drill that presently eats up so much of the hearing-impaired child's learning time.

Learning to use Signed English is no easy task. But the considerable effort to master it will be far outweighed by the enthusiastic response of your students and your newly buttressed competencies as a teacher.

Karen Luczak Saulnier
Teacher of the Hearing Impaired

Signed English for the Classroom

Introduction

This small reference book is the only one in the Signed English series which has been prepared especially for you, the classroom teacher. The other works in this series are designed for home and classroom and for use by parent and child, as well as by the teacher. In common with our other teaching aids, these sign words and phrases have been compiled to meet your immediate needs. We have tried to provide you in a convenient form the phrases and words you would need for a typical classroom day. Much of the vocabulary, of course, is useful in later grades.

This work differs in format and organization from our other books. First, we have reluctantly sacrificed graphic appeal and story line in order to include more material in a compact space. Under no circumstance would we do this for parents and children since we consider pleasure and warmth a necessary condition of language development and communication. Second, we have grouped vocabulary on a functional basis so that you can become aware of other sign words dealing with related ideas, objects, etc. Ordinarily, we avoid presenting lists of sign words. Connected discourse is usually a far superior medium for language learning. For those of you who are learning or improving your Signed English, we urge that you always use one or more of the carrier phrases included in each section while adding to your vocabulary. In this way you will properly overlearn the carrier phrase and more quickly learn to sign parallel to your natural speech rhythm. You might find our poetry and song books particularly useful in this regard. Until you are able to sign this way, you have not really mastered this technique.

It may be helpful to the teacher new to manual communication to describe the purpose and nature of Signed English. Signed English is an educational tool. It is a manual signal which is a reasonable semantic parallel to spoken English. It should be used with speech. The basic reason you use Signed English is so that a child can better learn English.

Ideally, Signed English should be introduced into the home and into the classroom as early in the child's life as possible. Since the amount of time that a child spends at home is much greater than that spent in class, maximum language exposure would normally occur in the home. For a variety of reasons, this is often impractical. In such cases, you have no choice but to be the prime language source. But you should spare no effort in continuing to try to involve the child's family in providing a rich language environment.

Each of the sign words in Signed English parallels the meaning of a separate word entry in a standard English dictionary. Sign words do not represent sounds or spelling. Similarly, the sign markers represent the meaning of a selected set of word form changes. Markers and sign words were selected because of frequent use with and by the preschool child. You must anticipate that it will take a long time before the child uses all the markers correctly. We know of no validated strategy for building up or adding markers other than to use all of the markers consistently and allow the child to learn them.*

Later in life, the deaf child will need to depend upon books to increase his English language competence. It will be helpful to him if he comes to regard books as a source of pleasure. Consequently, the teaching aids which are an integral part of the Signed English system should be readily available to each child in his home and in his class. The more they can enjoy and prize these books early in life, the more likely they are to turn to books again later.

Since sign words parallel the meaning of spoken words, the sign words pictured in this and in our other teaching aids do not stand for or represent the letters of the English alphabet. We show a right handed signer signing to you. He, first, executes a sign word and, second, when necessary, adds one of the sign markers. As you look at the signer, the marker is shown on his right as he would make it and appears on your left. This "mirror image" may confuse you a little at first, but you can orient yourself by turning the book upside-down and sighting down the signer's body. The one sign marker which is made before the sign word (the prefix for opposite—in, un, im, etc.,) is shown directly beneath the chin. In short, the markers are all shown opposite the left-right sequence of print because you are looking at a signer and because we treat each sign word as a discrete entity.

Signed English is not a language. It is not a substitute for the American Sign Language. It is neither better nor worse than the American Sign Language. It was

---

*Some parents do not handle English well enough to use all of the sign markers. We recommend that they use a reduced, but consistent, set of seven markers. They should use one past and one plural: the irregulars. They can also drop the "opposite" prefix, the comparative, the superlative, the participle, and the agent. Of course, if this were the only language that the child were exposed to, this would necessarily limit the child's language competence.

designed for a different purpose. The basic reason you see the American Sign Language is to communicate with users of that language. Signed English resembles the American Sign Language primarily because the over- whelming majority of the signs are taken from the American Sign Language. When a sign "enters" the Signed English system it becomes the semantic equiva- lent of one given English word. Much of the time, the sign and the sign word have the same meaning. Some- times they do not. Moreover, sign order and structural characteristics differ as well and these differences make for further difference in meaning. This is nothing to be alarmed about. Children all over the world can and do learn more than one spoken language even though most of the phonemic elements of the different languages are the same. Usually, they learn the two languages from systematic exposure to each. There is no reason that we know of that should prevent a child from dealing com- petently with two visual codes.

Occasionally you will encounter a different sign from that shown here for a given English word. Essentially, such a difference arises because the source language for the system, the American Sign Language, has different regional dialects and is a living, changing language. It has regional variations and synonyms. Another reason is that another system maker has invented an attractive sign. It is difficult to represent all of these signs graphi- cally in one sign system. However, it is possible and very desirable that you, the teacher, simply accept such alternate signs as you would synonyms in English. We suggest that you treat the signs in Signed English as pre- ferred and regard other signs for the same word as acceptable synonyms. In actual fact, the number of words for which there are more than one sign is not very large.

Since Signed English has been designed to serve purposes somewhat similar to those intended for Seeing Essential English, Signing Exact English, and Linguis- tics of Visual English, it may be useful to point out some of the major differences between Signed English and these other systems. In essence, these systems use signs from the American Sign language to represent English words and word parts which have been sorted accord- ing to an arbitrary combination of sound, spelling, and meaning. Because sound is foreign to signs, because English spelling has only a tangential relationship to signs, and because complex and compound English words only sometimes have component Sign parallels, these systems contain opposing requirements which are difficult to reconcile. Further, these systems try to in-

clude a complete and fully differentiated set of significant word parts, i.e., prefixes and suffixes, which can be used in unlimited combination. Signed English, on the other hand, employs a *minimum* set of specific and class markers intended to signal the *meaning* of the most common word form changes. Moreover, only one mark- er can be used in combination with a sign word. In effect, Signed English is as simple a system as can be devised to meet the basic needs of young children, their parents, and their teachers. The system is supplemented with the manual alphabet when the child's language base is sufficiently large for him to handle greater lan- guage complexity.

Finally, we want to emphasize that Signed English was *not* designed to replace other educational tools and techniques which have been used successfully with deaf children. Auditory training and speech training are es- sential elements in a comprehensive program for hearing- impaired children. Logically, a child who possesses a better language base should be more able to profit from such training than one with more limited language.

●

References

Bornstein, H., A description of some current sign systems designed to represent English, *American Annals of the Deaf*, 118 454-470 (1973).

Bornstein. H., Signed English: A manual approach to English lan- guage development, *Journal of Speech and Hearing Disorders*, Vol. 39, 330-343 (1974).

Bornstein, H., Saulnier, K. L., and Hamilton, L. B., *The Comprehensive Signed English Dictionary*. Washington, D.C., Gallaudet College Press (1983).

Bornstein, H., Sign language in the education of the deaf. In *Lan- guage of the Deaf: Psychological, Linguistics, and Sociological Per- spectives*, I. M. Schlesinger and L. Namir, (Eds.) New York, Aca- demic Press, Inc., 333-361 (1978).

Bornstein, H., Systems of sign. In *Hearing and Hearing Impairment*, L. Bradford and W. Hardy (Eds.) New York, Grune & Stratton, Inc., Ch. 12, 155-172 (1979).

Bornstein, H., The design of Signed English readers. *Proceedings of Gallaudet Conference on Reading in Relation to Deafness*, Wash- ington, D.C. (in press).

Goodman, L., Wilson, P. S., & Bornstein, H. Results of a national survey of sign language programs in special education. *Mental Re- tardation*, 1978, 16(2), 104-106.

Auditory Training

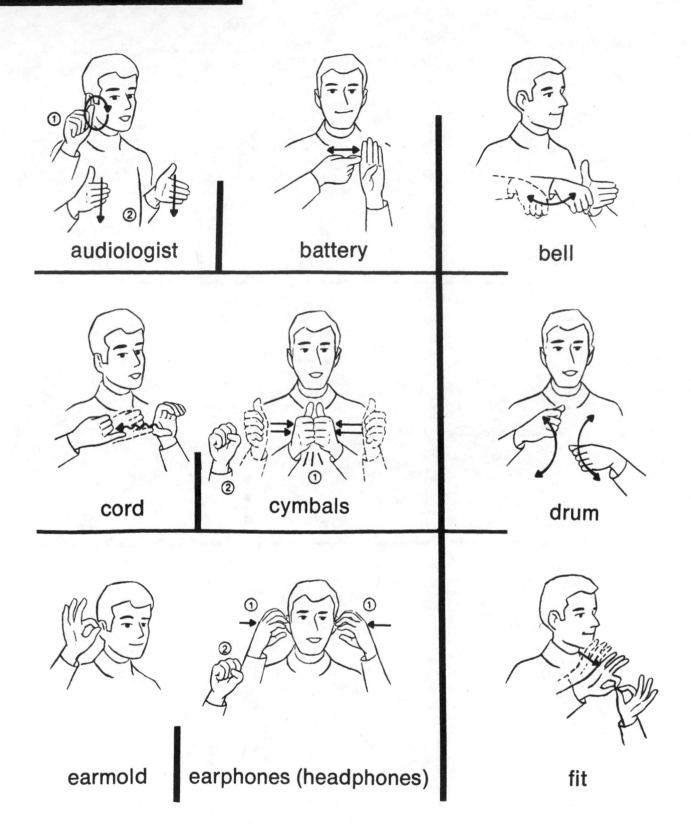

audiologist

battery

bell

cord

cymbals

drum

earmold

earphones (headphones)

fit

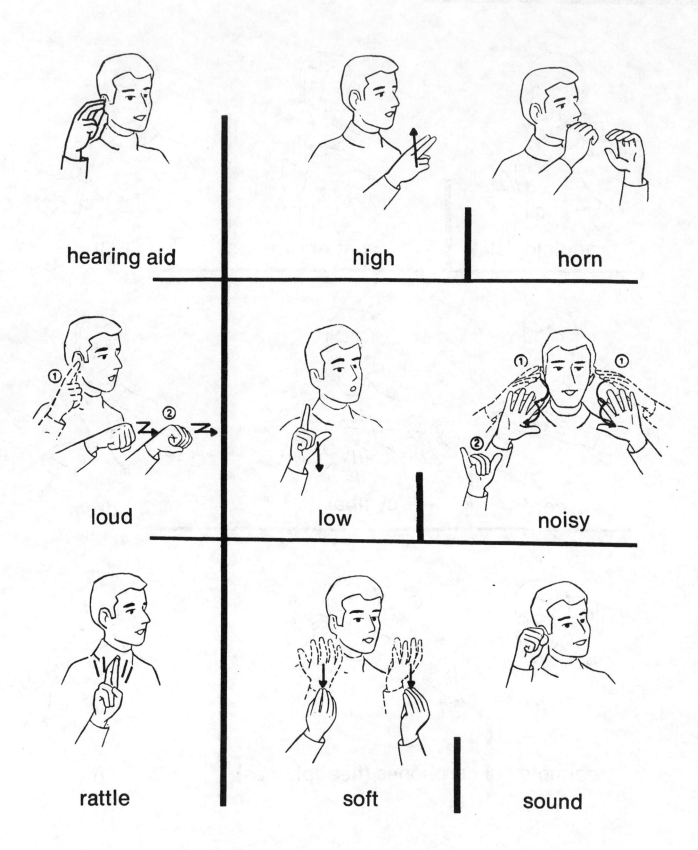

hearing aid

high

horn

loud

low

noisy

rattle

soft

sound

2

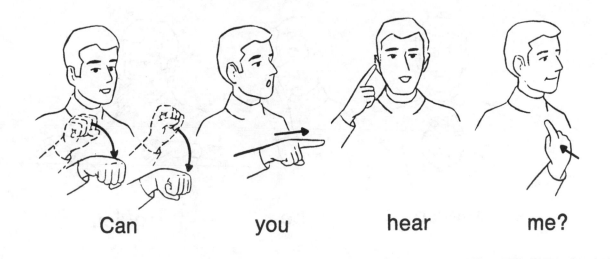

Can   you   hear   me?

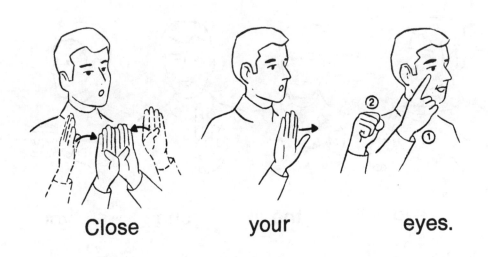

Close   your   eyes.

Listen____.

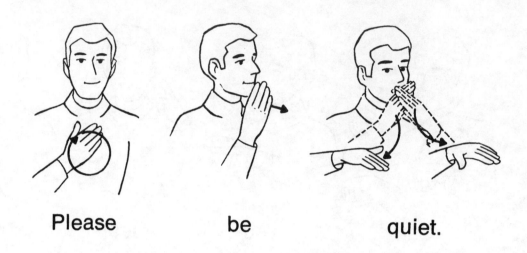

Please   be   quiet.

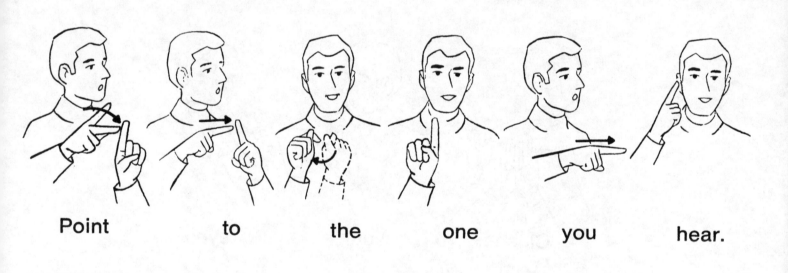

Point   to   the   one   you   hear.

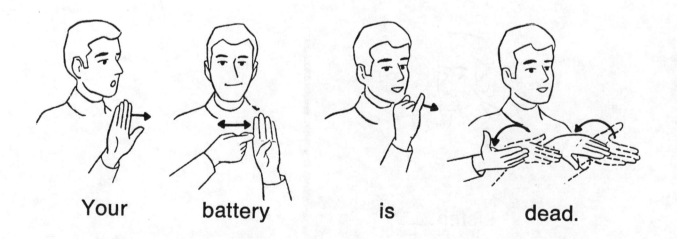

Your   battery   is   dead.

Calendar

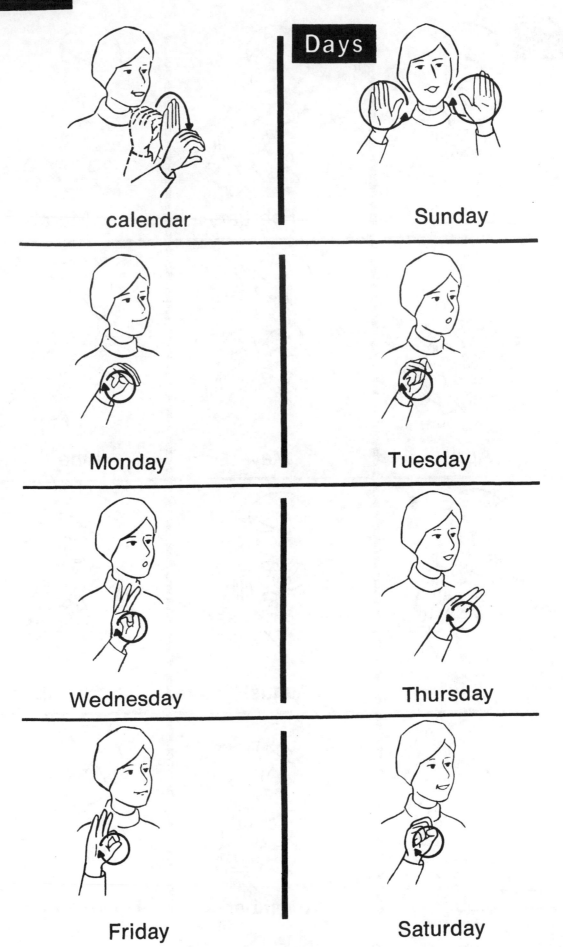

calendar

Sunday

Monday

Tuesday

Wednesday

Thursday

Friday

Saturday

5

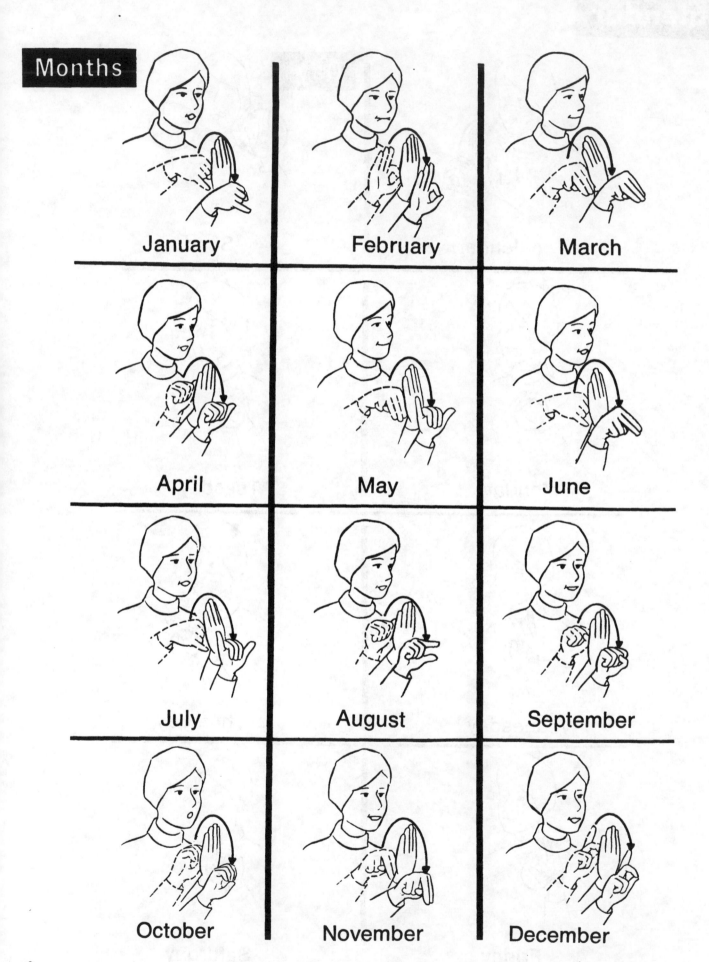

Months

| January | February | March |
| July | August | September |

April   May   June

October   November   December

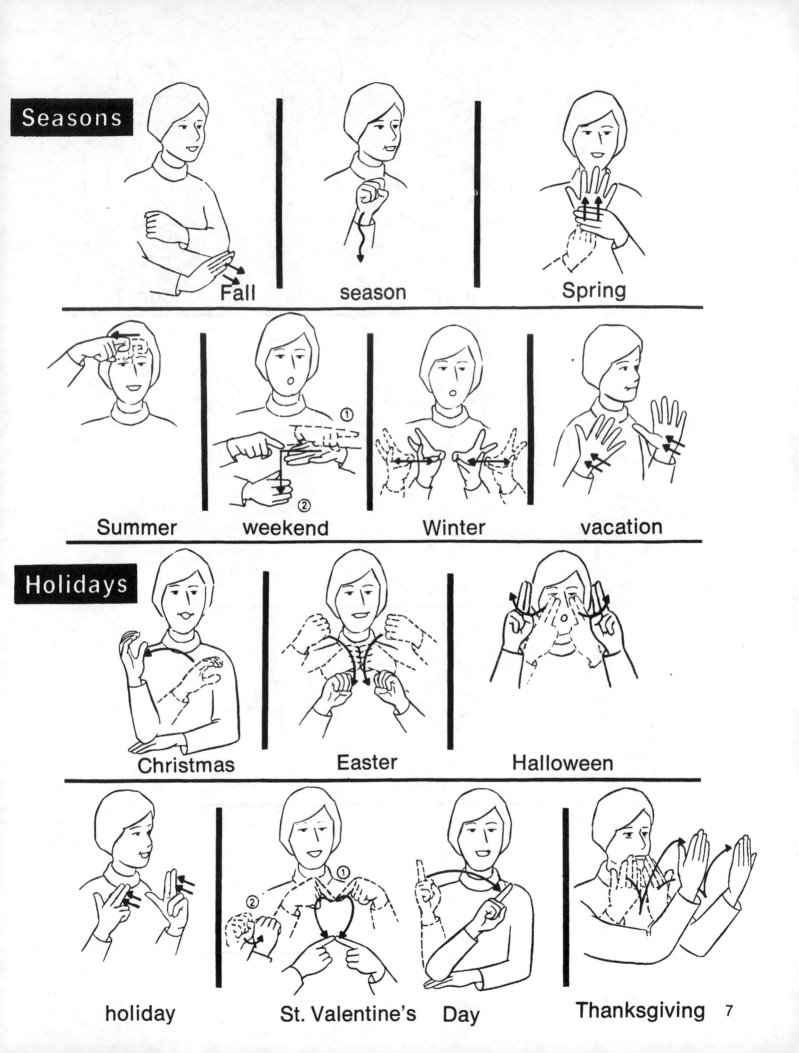

Seasons

Fall

season

Spring

Summer

weekend

Winter

vacation

Holidays

Christmas

Easter

Halloween

holiday

St. Valentine's Day

Thanksgiving 7

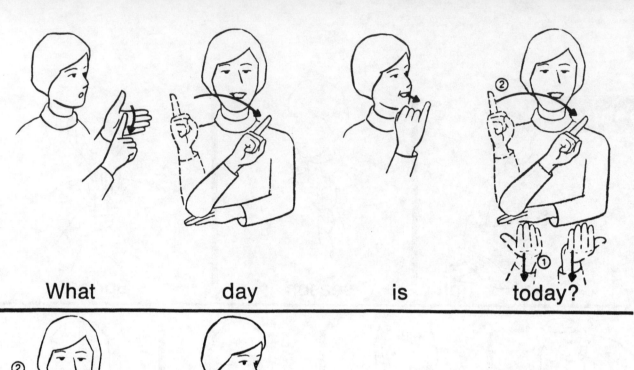

What	day	is	today?

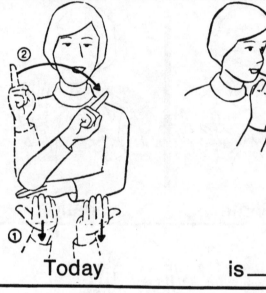

Today   is ___ .

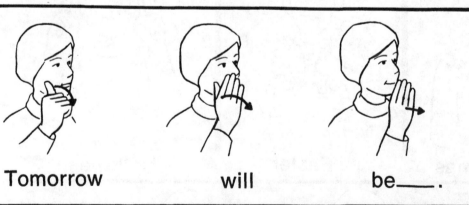

Tomorrow	will	be ___ .

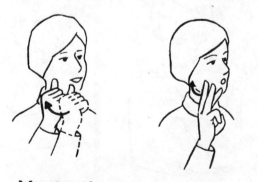

Yesterday   was ___ .

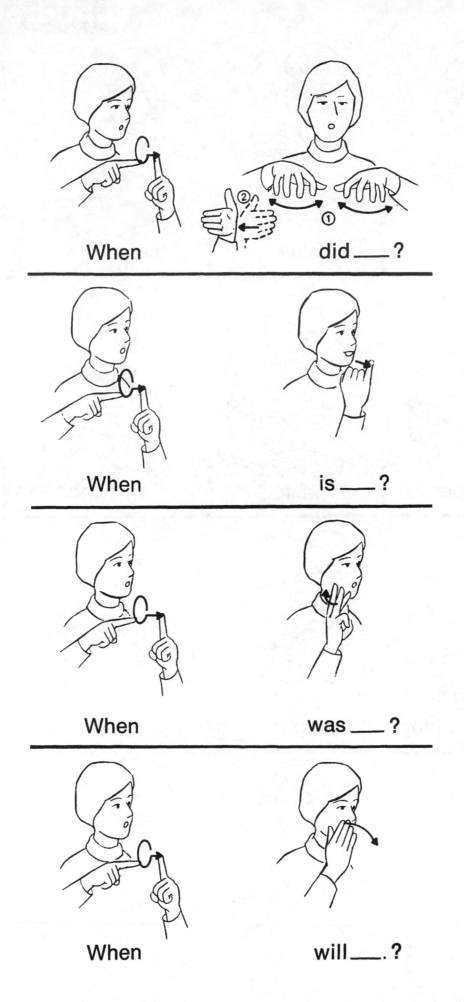

When   did ____?

When   is ____?

When   was ____?

When   will ____.?

9

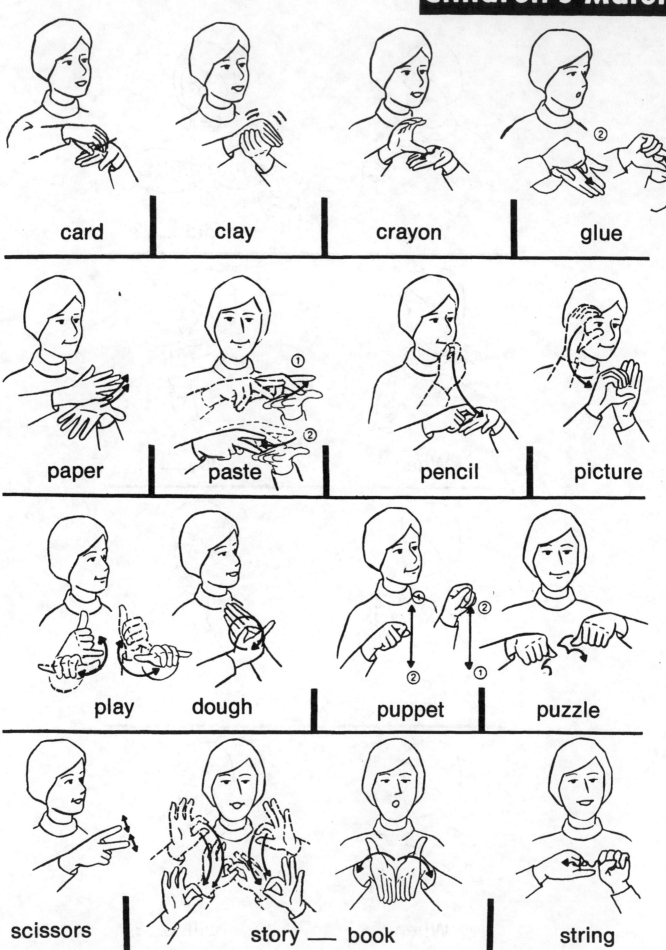

card

clay

crayon

glue

paper

paste

pencil

picture

play

dough

puppet

puzzle

scissors

story — book

string

Children's Phrases

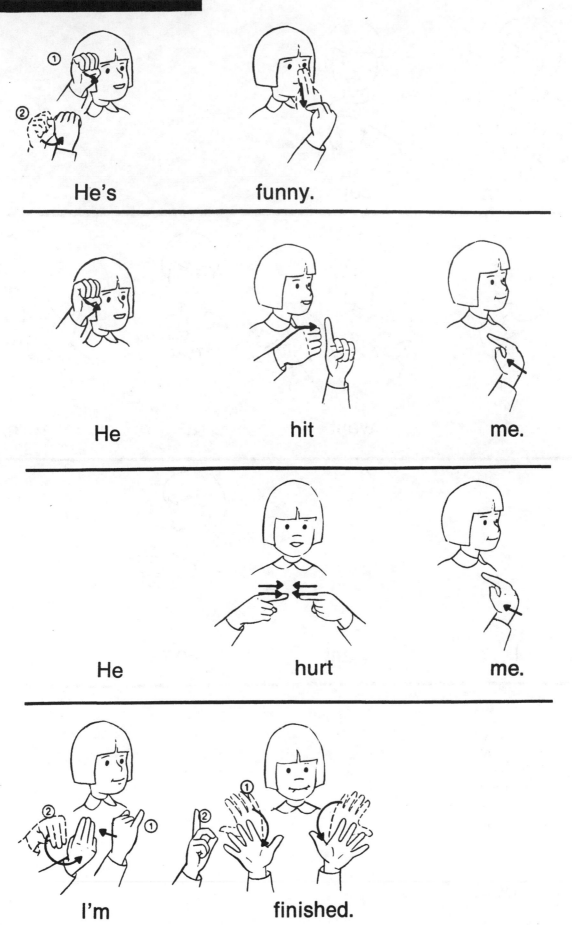

He's   funny.

He   hit   me.

He   hurt   me.

I'm   finished.

11

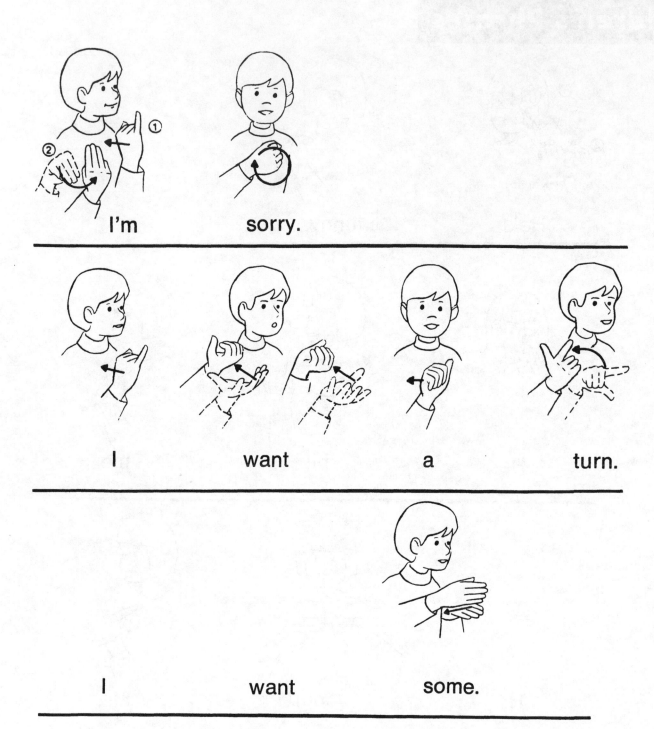

I'm   sorry.

I   want   a   turn.

I   want   some.

Look!

Classroom Items

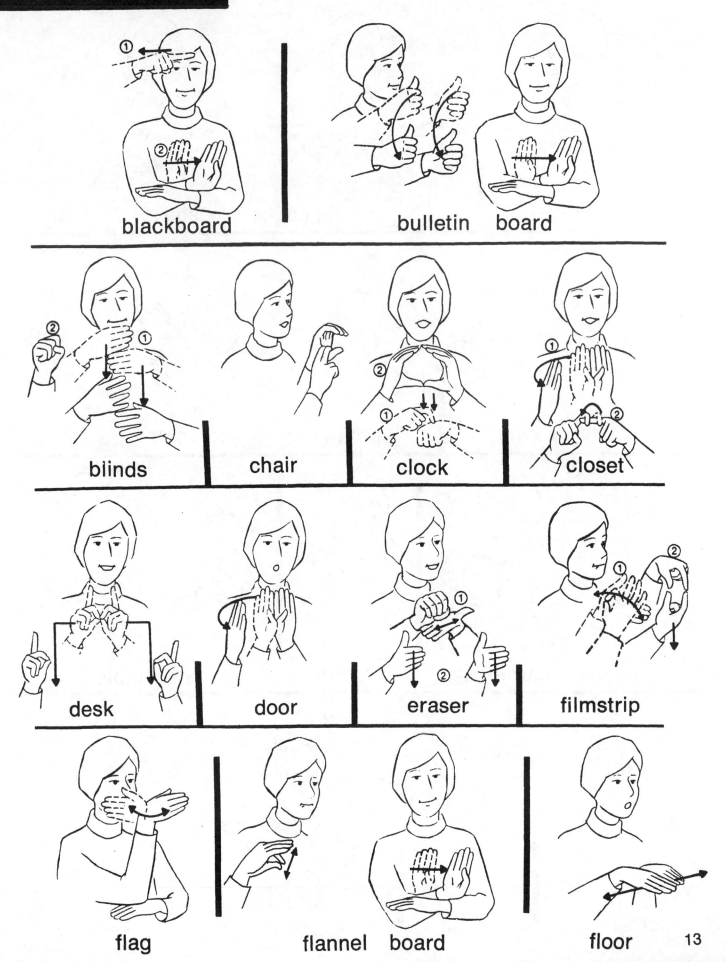

blackboard

bulletin board

blinds

chair

clock

closet

desk

door

eraser

filmstrip

flag

flannel board

floor

13

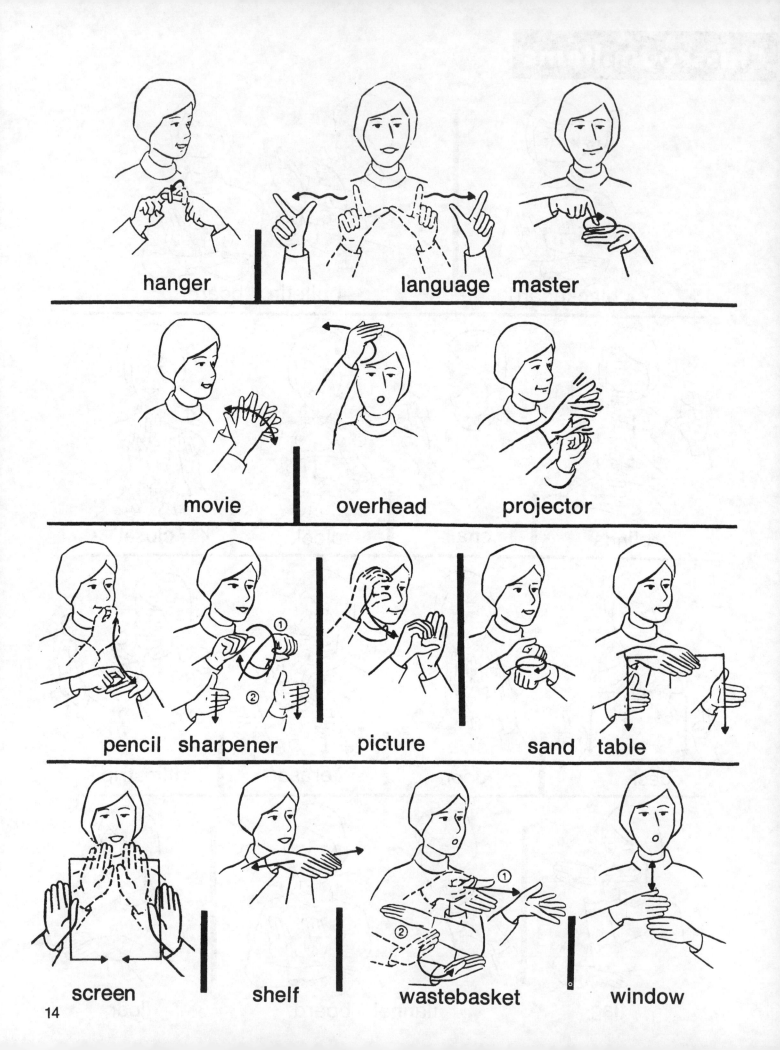

hanger

language   master

movie   overhead   projector

pencil   sharpener   picture   sand   table

screen   shelf   wastebasket   window

14

May   I   go   to   the   bathroom?

Move   over,   please.

She's   silly.

Stop!   No.

Thank   you.

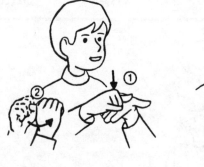     

That's   my   classroom.

That's   mine.

You're   welcome.

Classroom Phrases

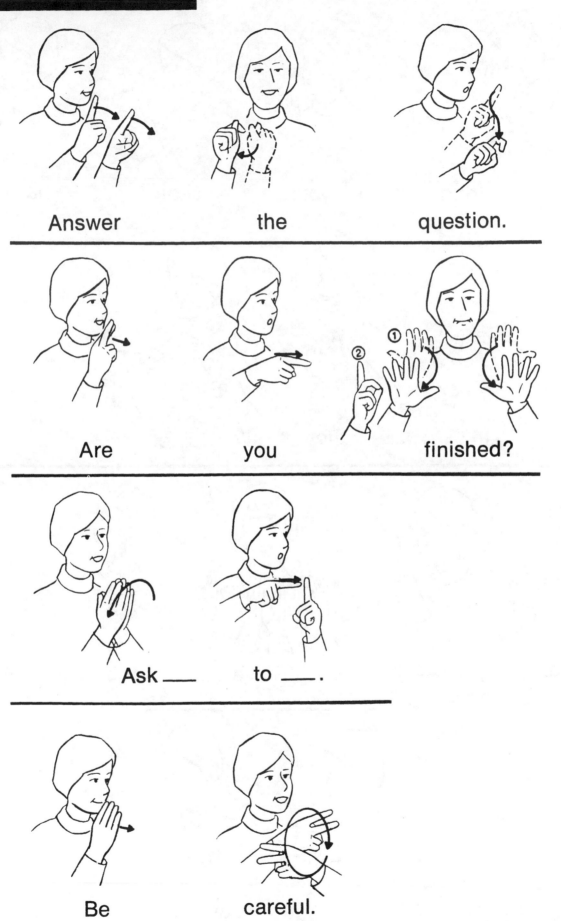

Answer   the   question.

Are   you   finished?

Ask ___   to ___ .

Be   careful.

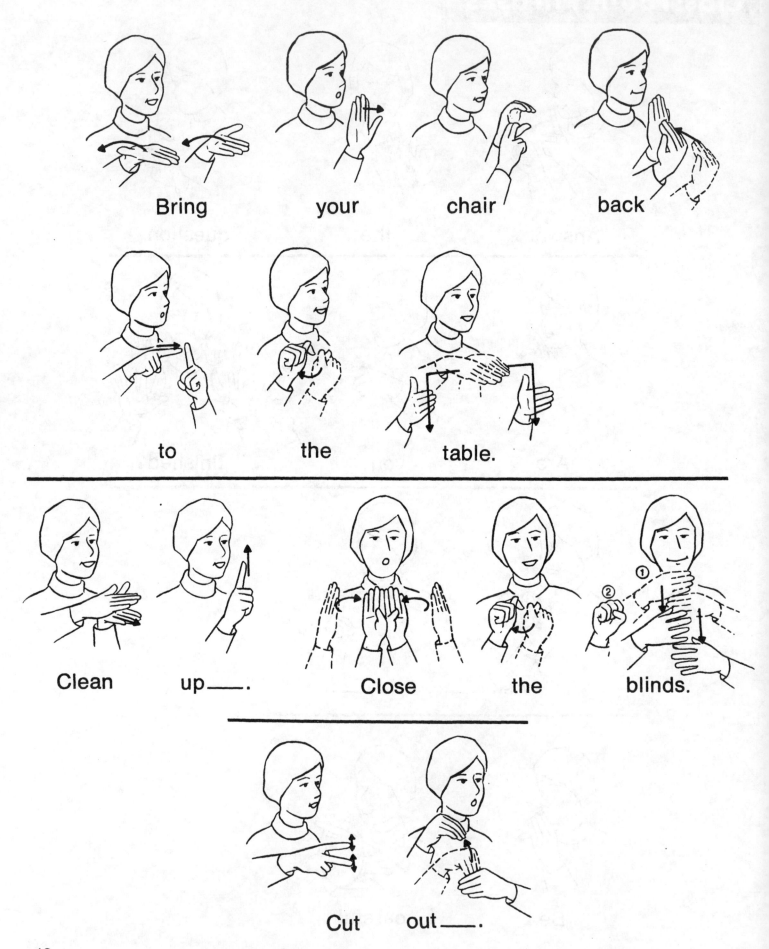

Bring your chair back

to the table.

Clean up____. Close the blinds.

Cut out____.

18

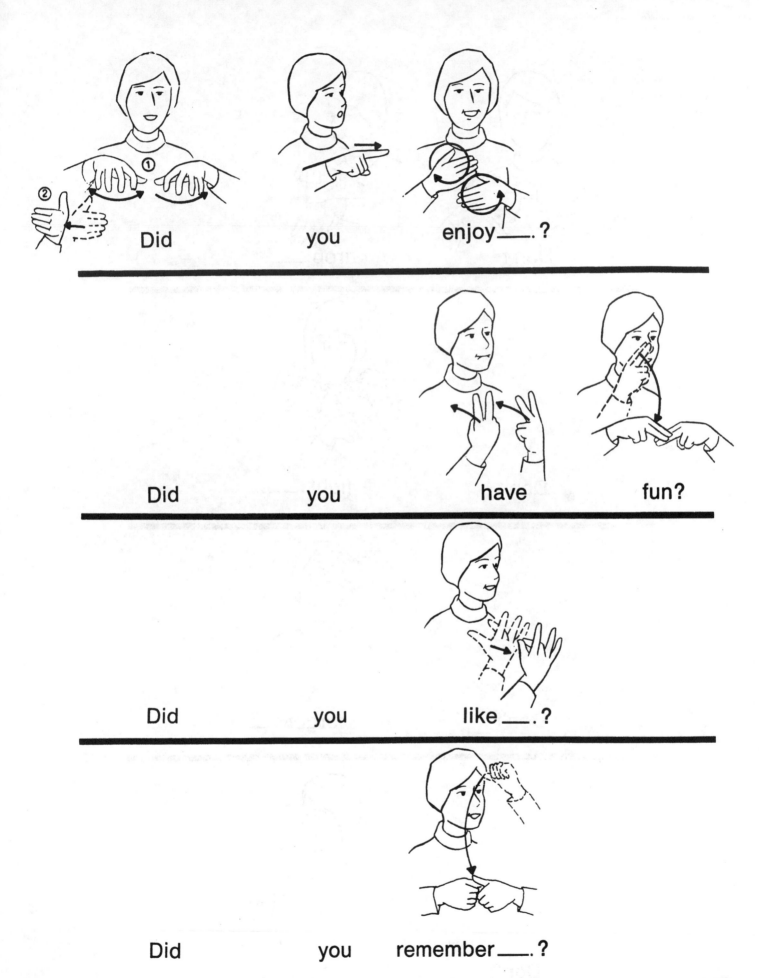

Did you enjoy ___ .?

Did you have fun?

Did you like ___ .?

Did you remember ___ .?

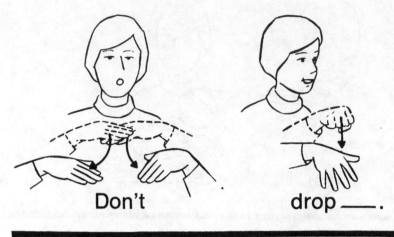

Don't   drop _____.

Don't   fight _____.

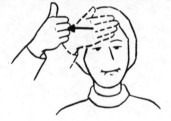

Don't   forget _____.

Don't   hit _____.

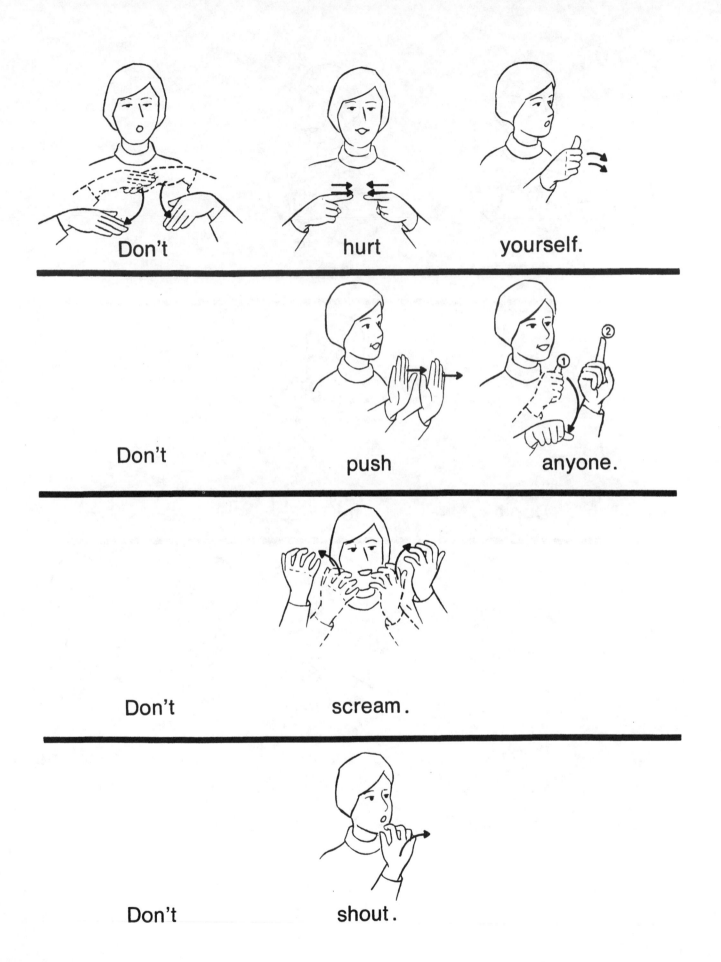

Don't   hurt   yourself.

Don't   push   anyone.

Don't   scream.

Don't   shout.

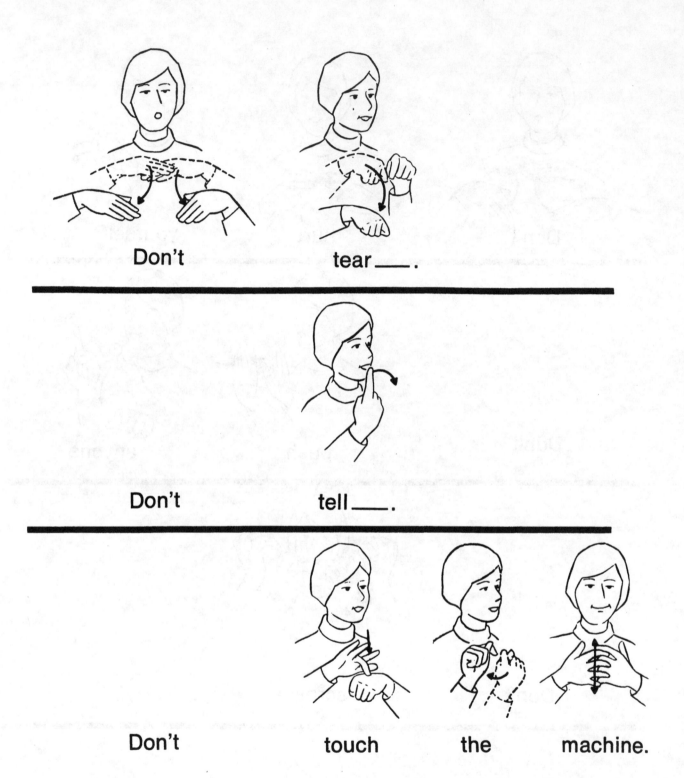

Don't   tear ___ .

Don't   tell ___ .

Don't   touch   the   machine.

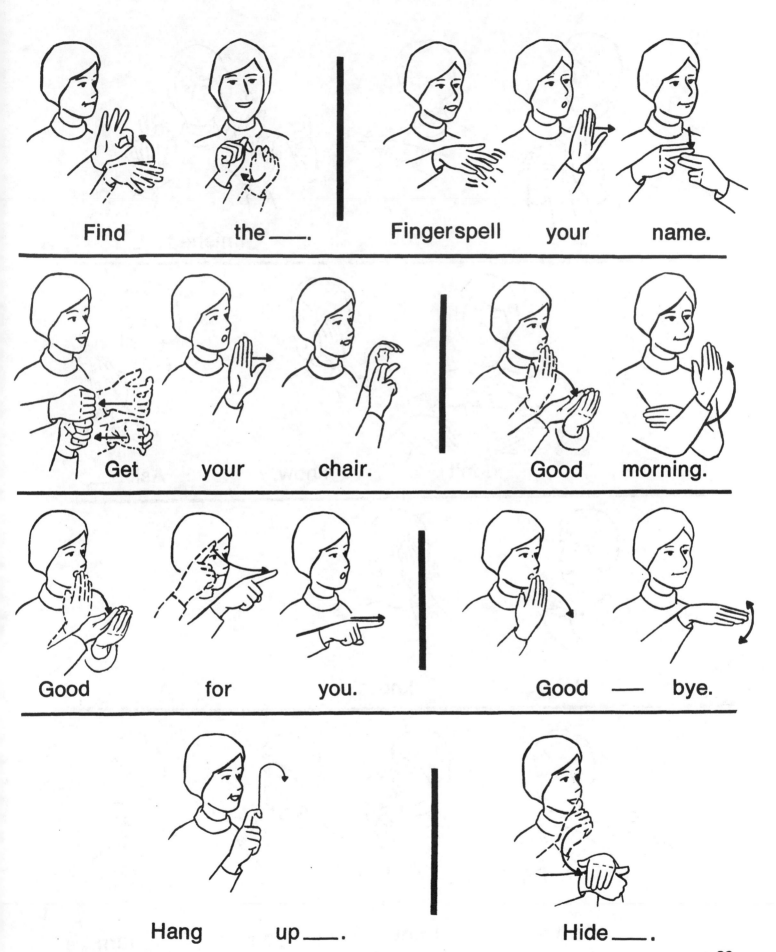

Find **the ___.** | **Fingerspell** **your** **name.**

Get **your** **chair.** | **Good** **morning.**

Good **for** **you.** | **Good** **—** **bye.**

Hang **up ___.** | **Hide ___.**

23

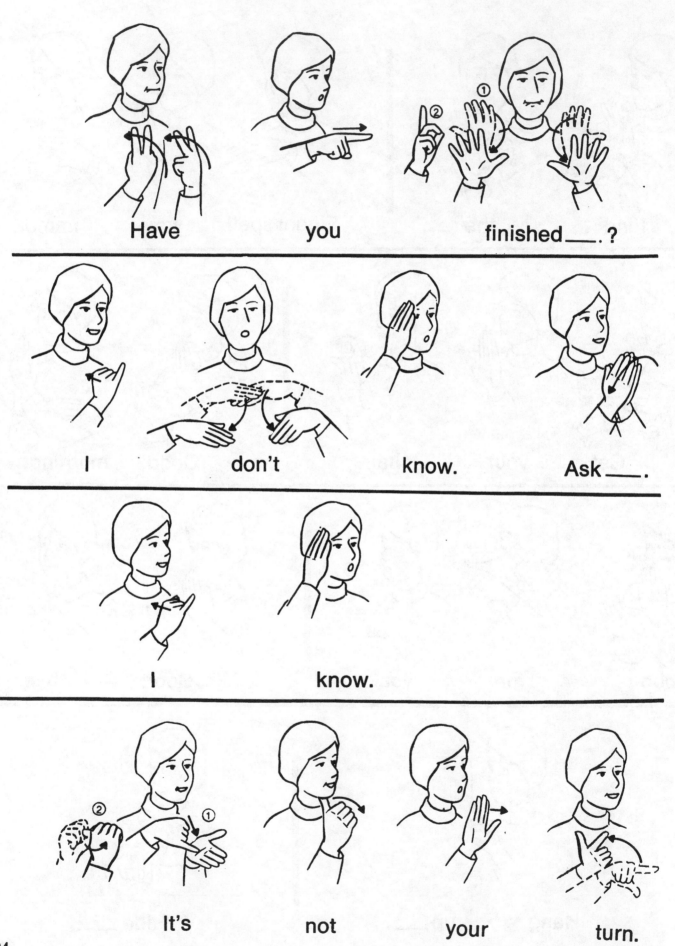

Have   you   finished ___.?

I   don't   know.   Ask ___.

I   know.

It's   not   your   turn.

24

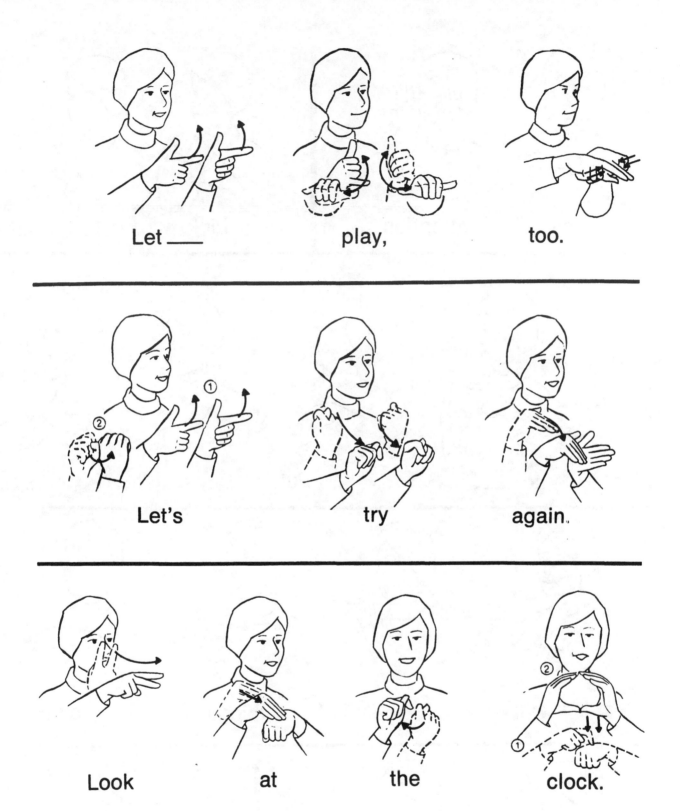

Let ___   play,   too.

Let's   try   again.

Look   at   the   clock.

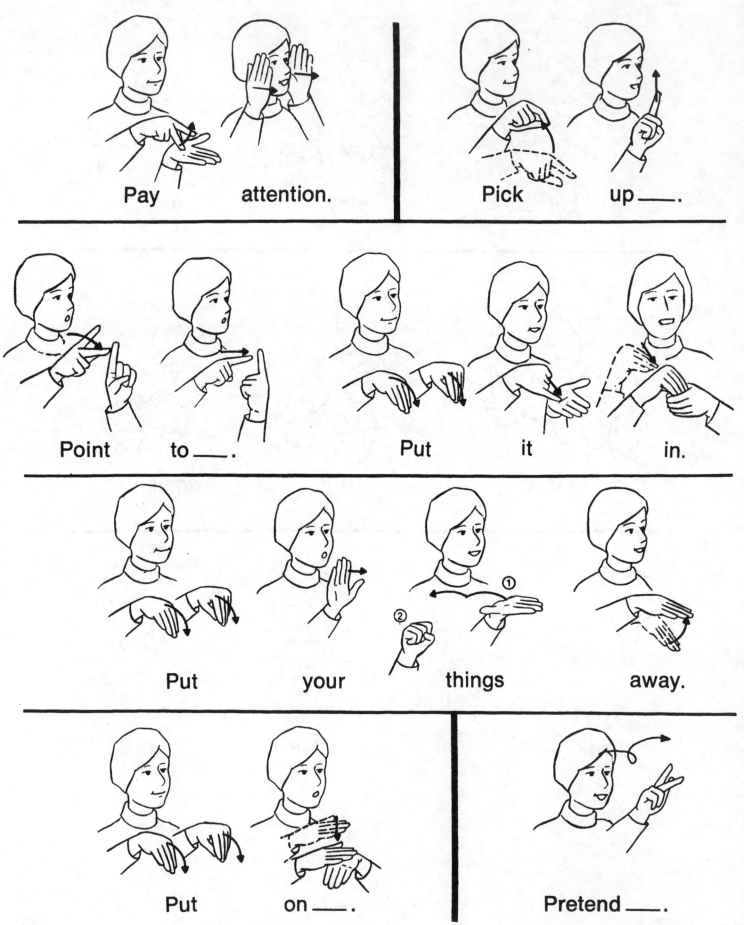

Pay   attention.   Pick   up ___.

Point   to ___.   Put   it   in.

Put   your   things   away.

Put   on ___.   Pretend ___.

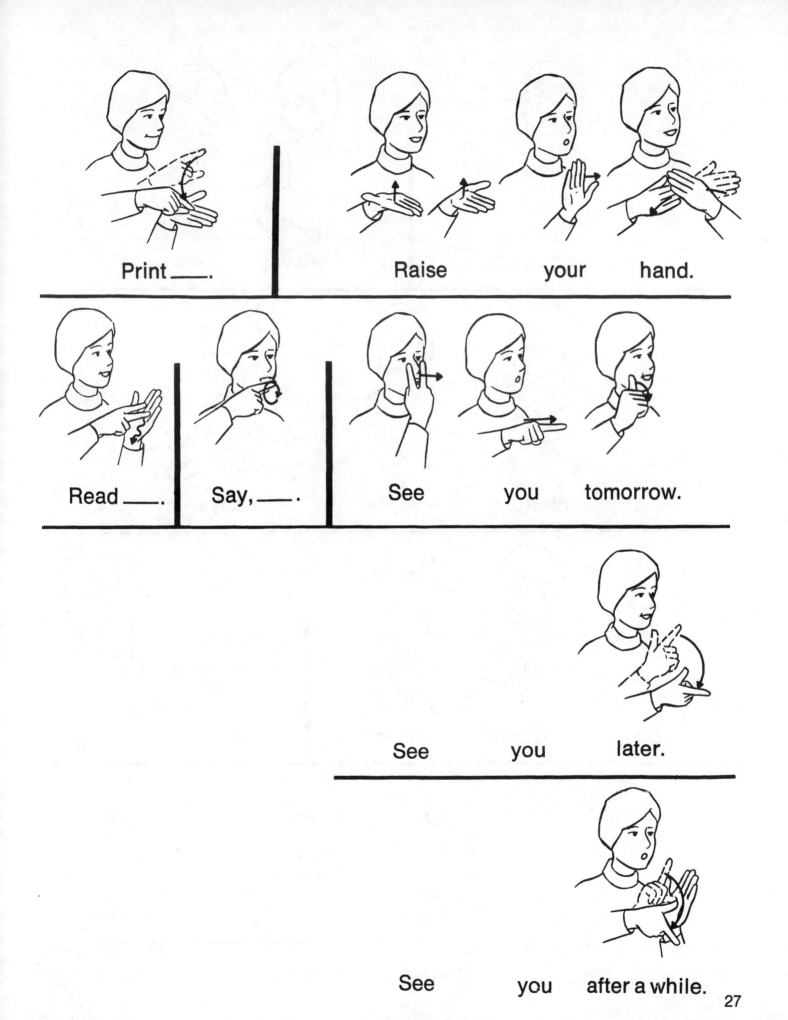

Print ____.

Raise your hand.

Read ____.

Say, ____.

See you tomorrow.

See you later.

See you after a while.

27

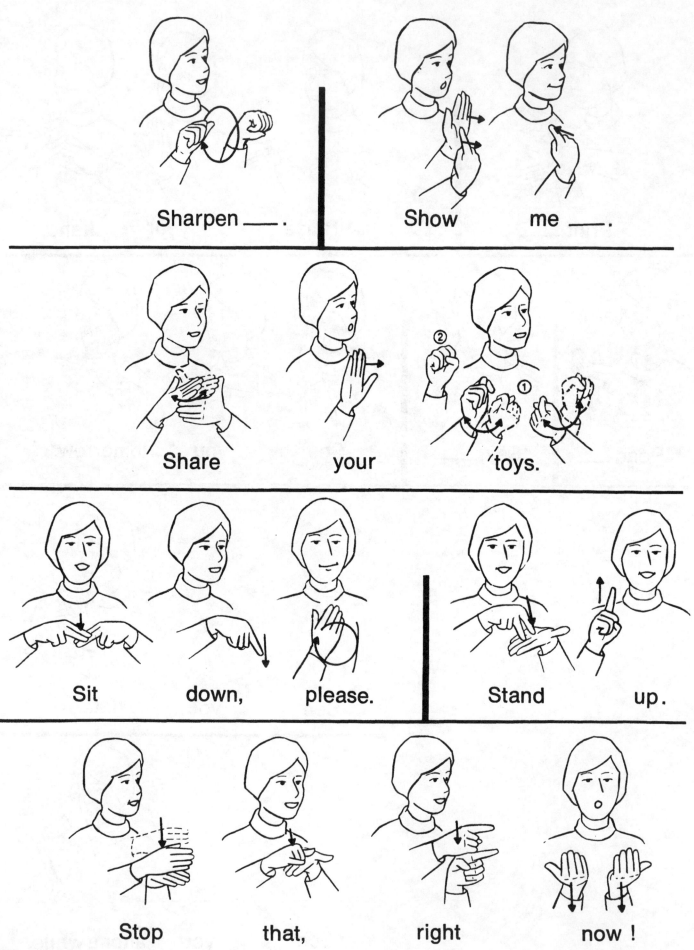

Sharpen ___.

Show me ___.

Share your toys.

Sit down, please.

Stand up.

Stop that, right now !

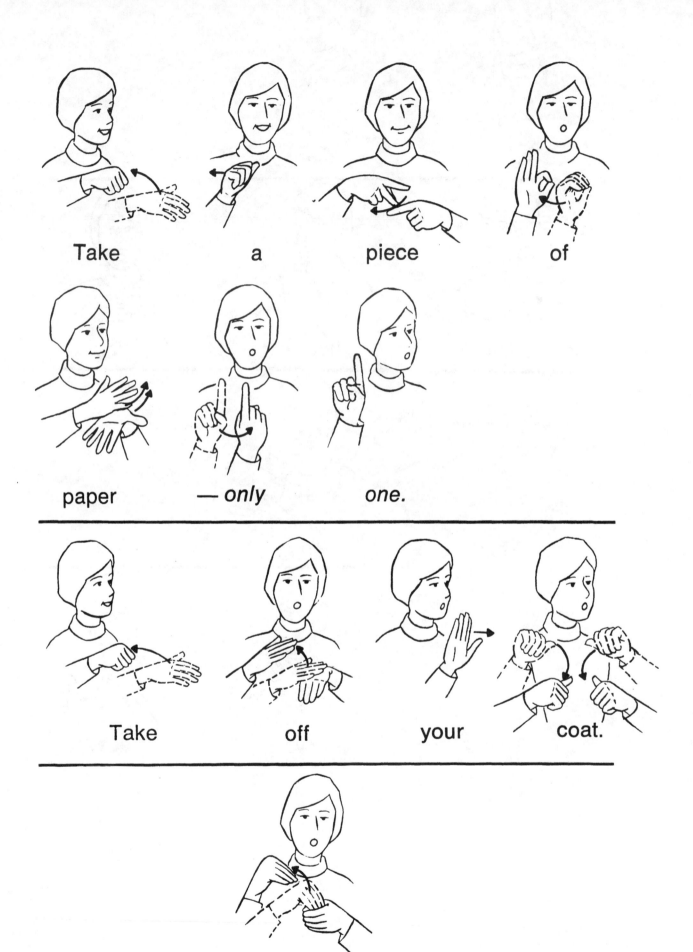

Take   a   piece   of

paper   *— only*   *one.*

Take   off   your   coat.

Take   out

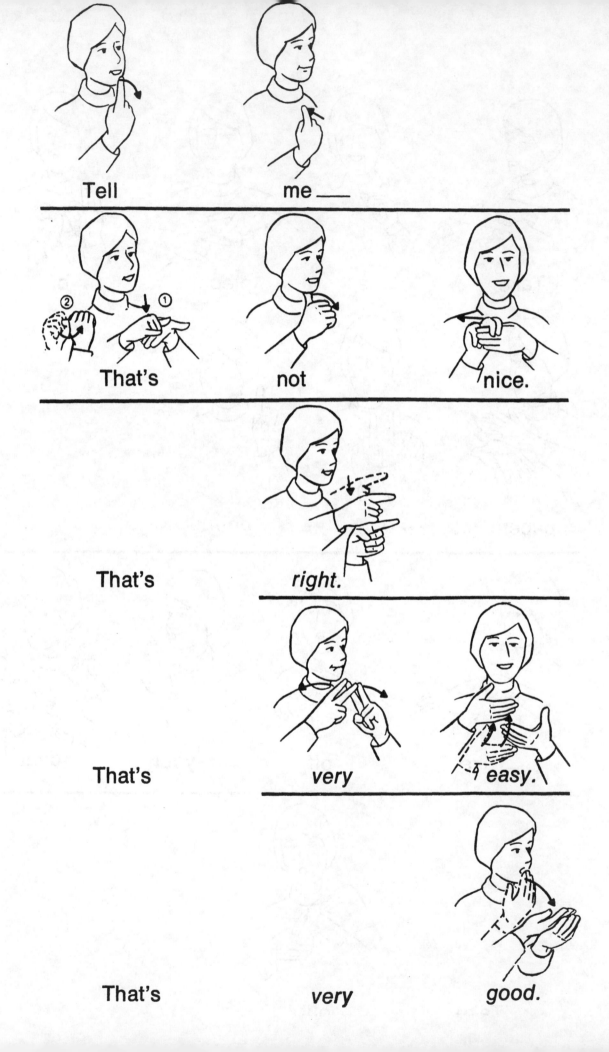

Tell   me ___

That's   not   nice.

That's   *right.*

That's   *very*   *easy.*

That's   *very*   *good.*

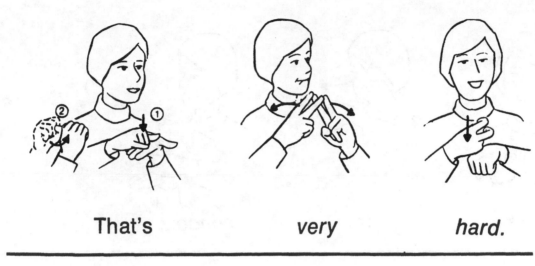

That's	*very*	*hard.*

That's	*wrong.*

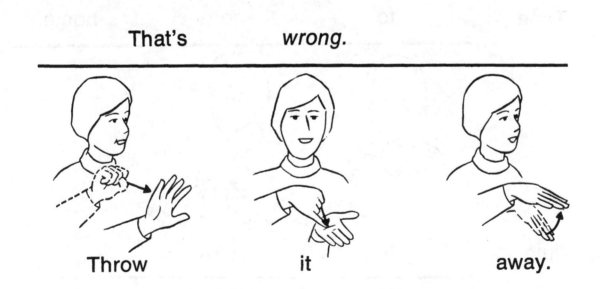

Throw	it	away.

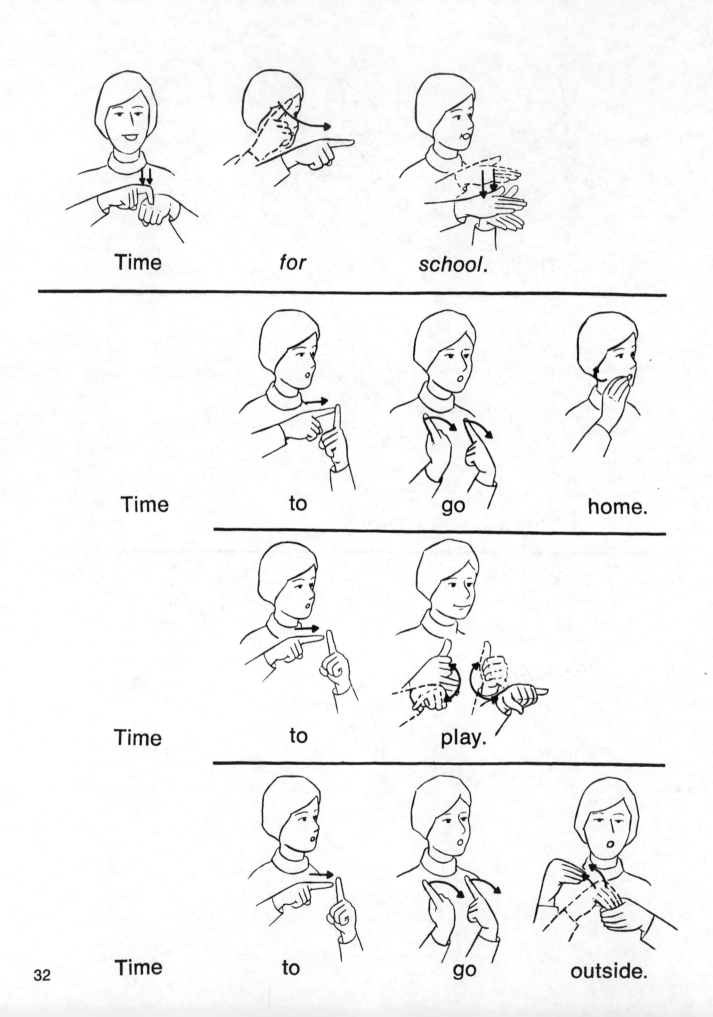

Time   *for*   *school.*

Time   to   go   home.

Time   to   play.

Time   to   go   outside.

Turn   off   the   lights.

Turn   on   _____, again.

Wait!

Watch   me,   please.

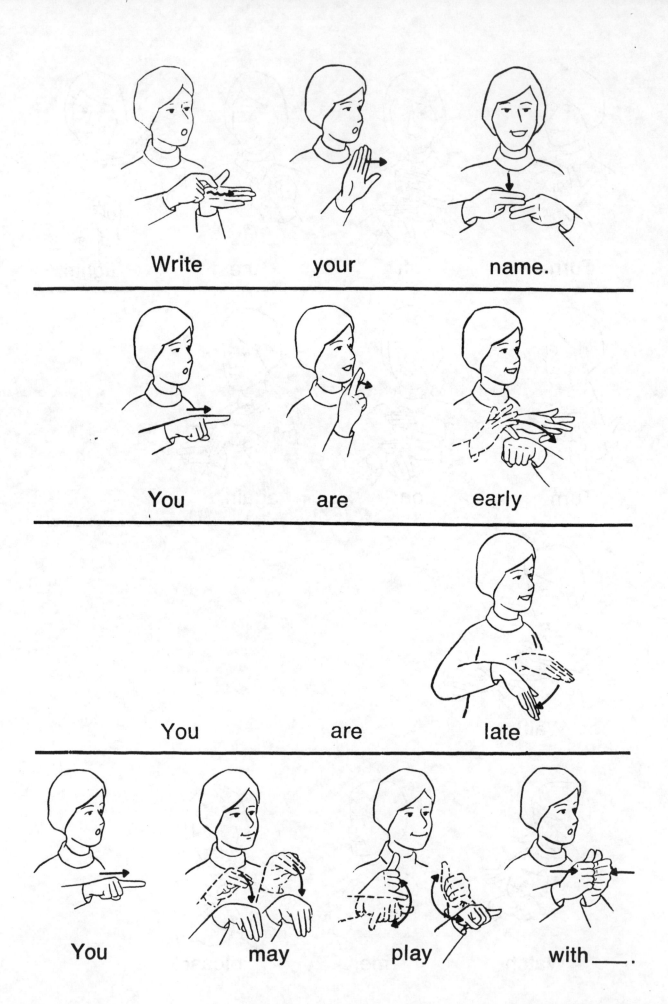

Write   your   name.

You   are   early

You   are   late

You   may   play   with____.

Music and Rhythms

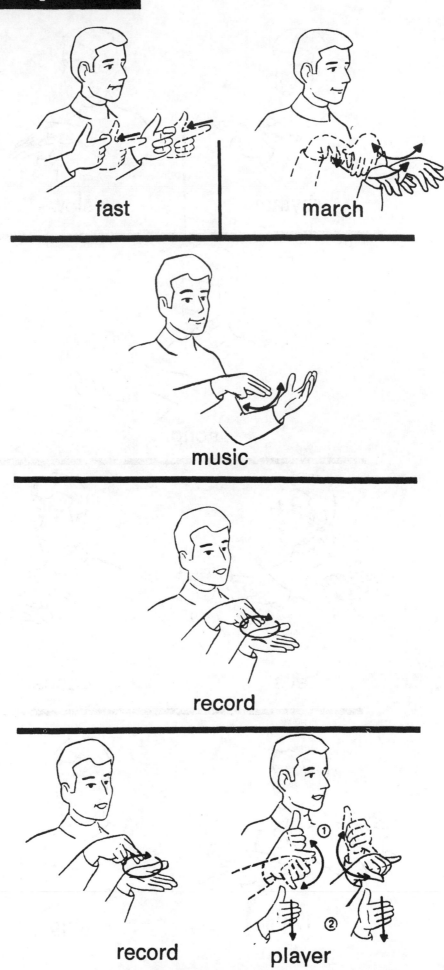

fast

march

music

record

record

player

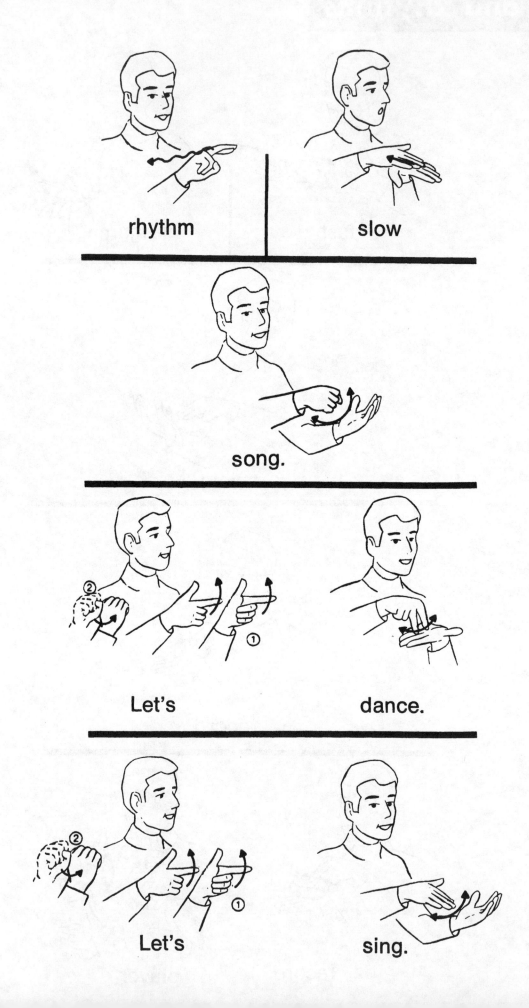

rhythm

slow

song.

Let's

dance.

Let's

sing.

Numbers and Coins

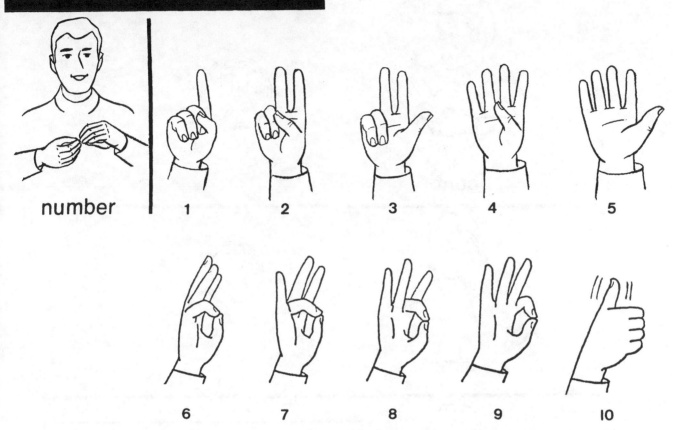

number   1   2   3   4   5

6   7   8   9   10

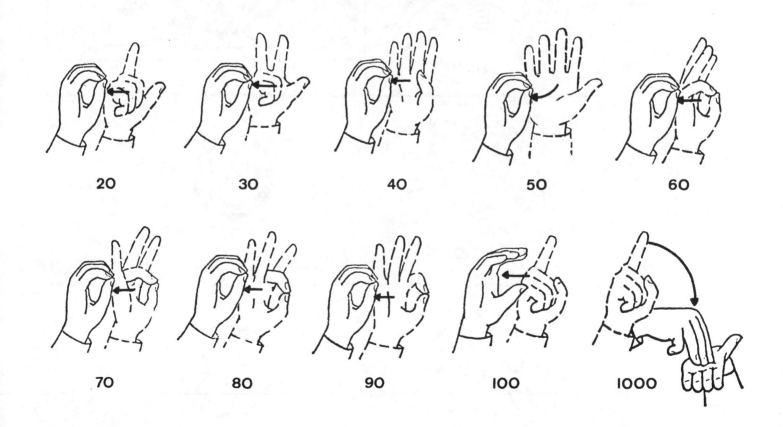

20   30   40   50   60

70   80   90   100   1000

cent

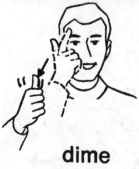

dime

dollar

nickel

quarter

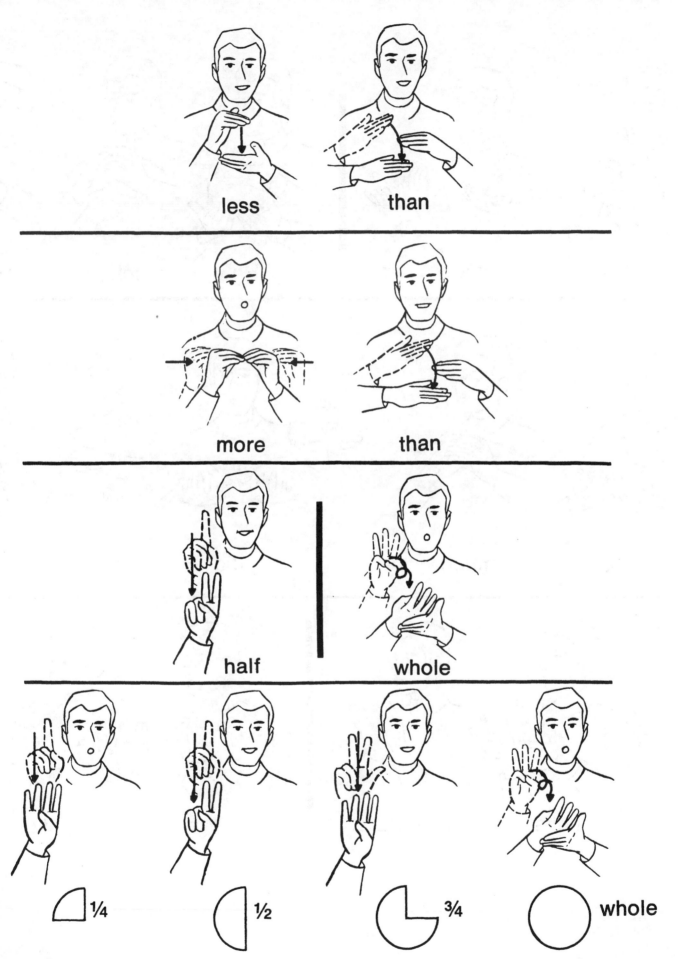

less   than

more   than

half | whole

¼   ½   ¾   whole

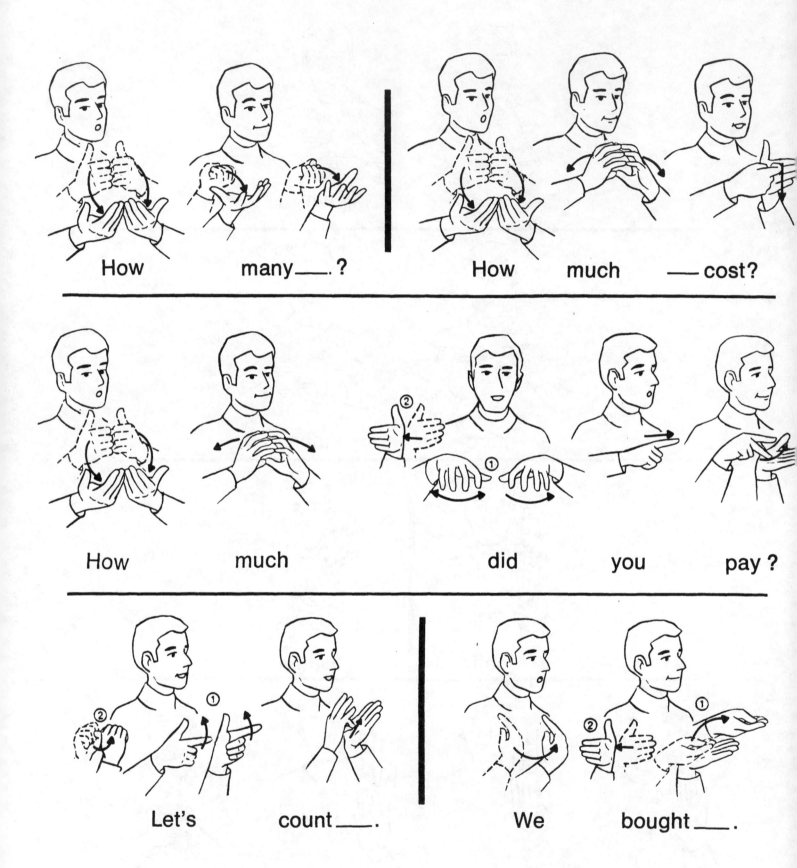

How   many___.?   How   much   —cost?

How   much   did   you   pay ?

Let's   count___.   We   bought___.

Painting

black

blue

brown

gold

green

grey

orange

pink

purple

red

yellow

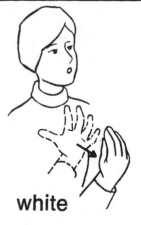

white

41

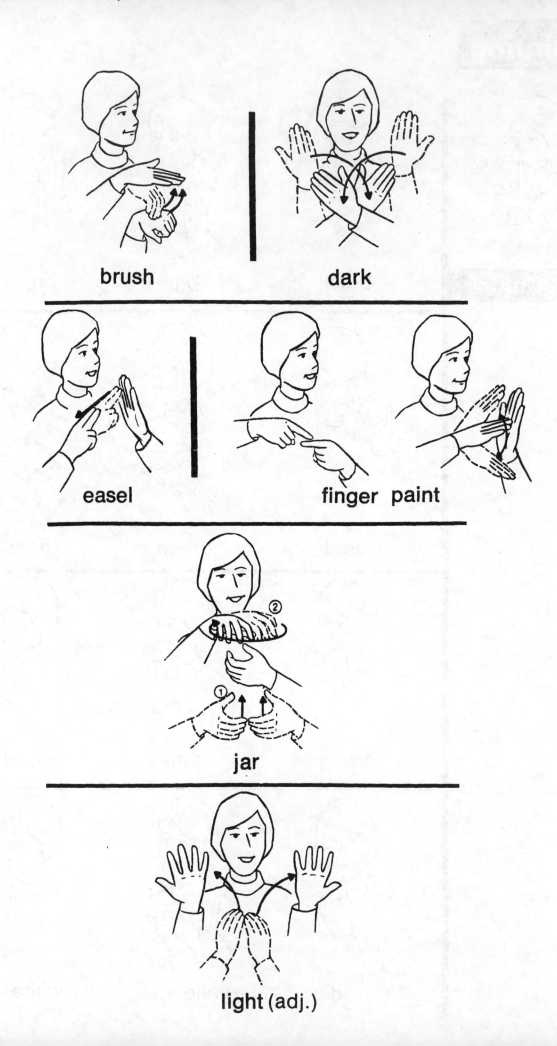

brush

dark

easel

finger paint

jar

light (adj.)

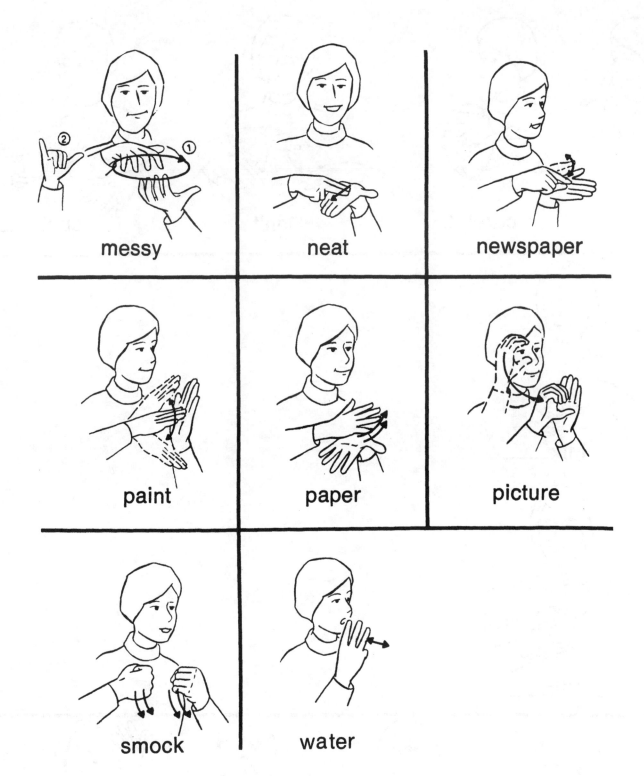

messy

neat

newspaper

paint

paper

picture

smock

water

43

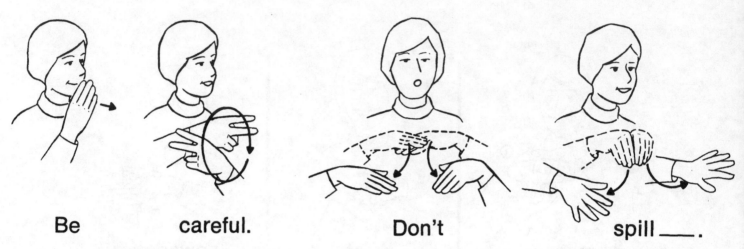

Be   careful.   Don't   spill ____.

Mix____.

Stir____.

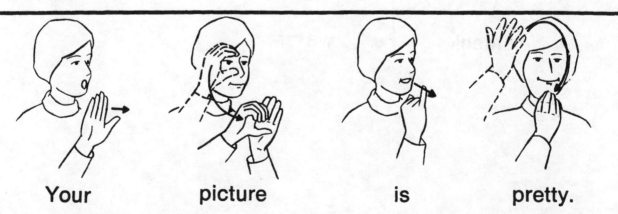

Your   picture   is   pretty.

Question Forms

Can ___ ?

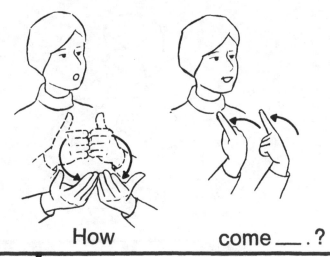

How   come ___ . ?

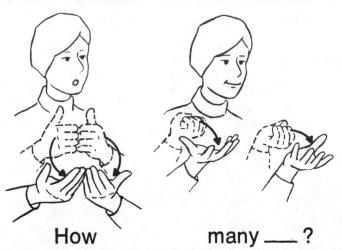

How   many ___ ?

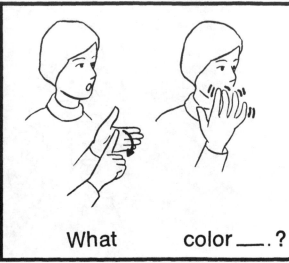

What   color ___ . ?

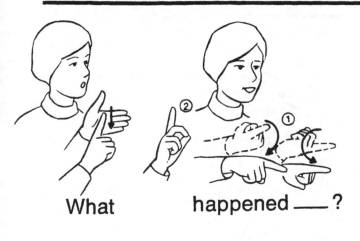

What   happened ___ ?

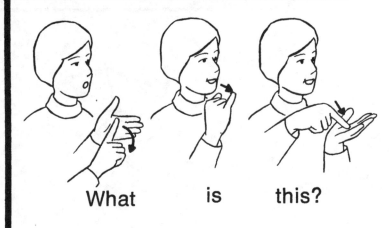

What   is   this?

What   is   that?   45

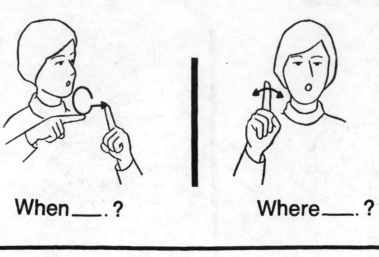

When ___ . ?   Where ___ . ?

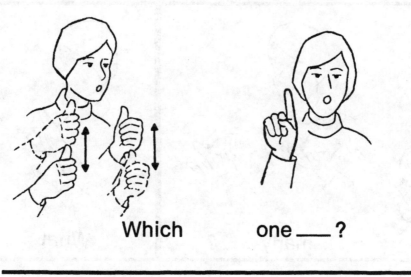

Which   one ___ ?

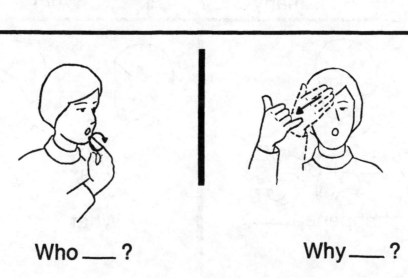

Who ___ ?   Why ___ ?

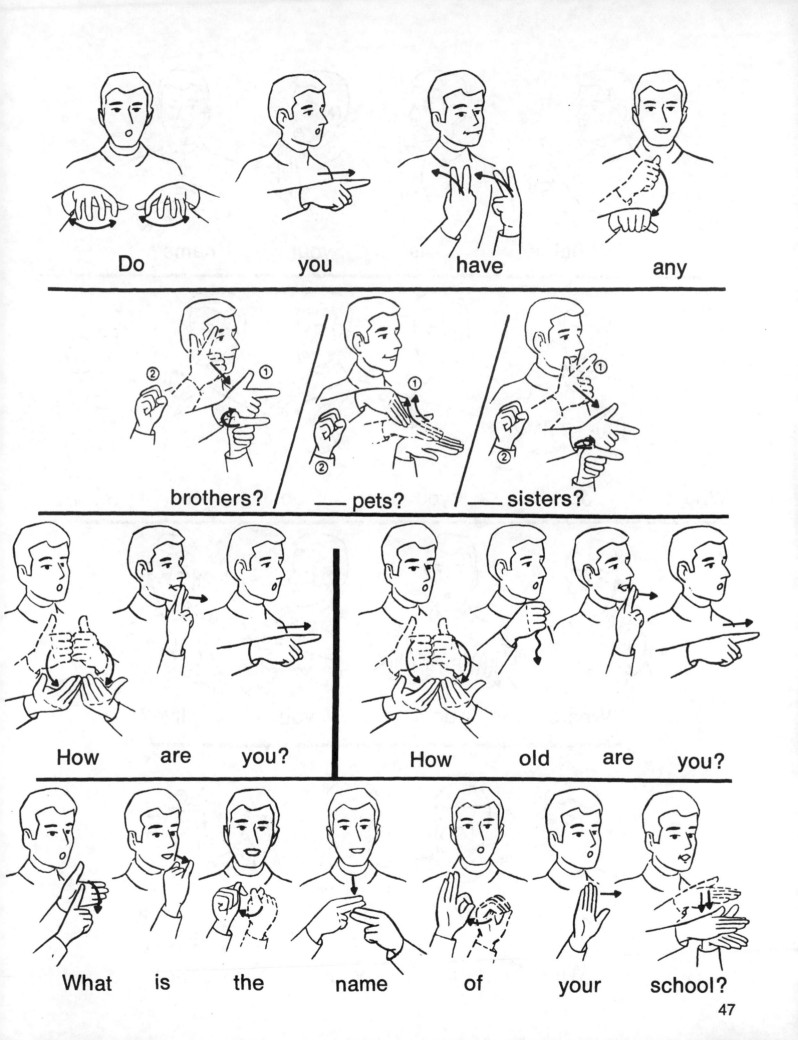

Do you have any

brothers? ____ pets? ____ sisters?

How are you? How old are you?

What is the name of your school?

What   is   your   name?

Where   do   you   go   to   school?

Where   do   you   live?

Who   is   your   teacher?

Sequence Activities

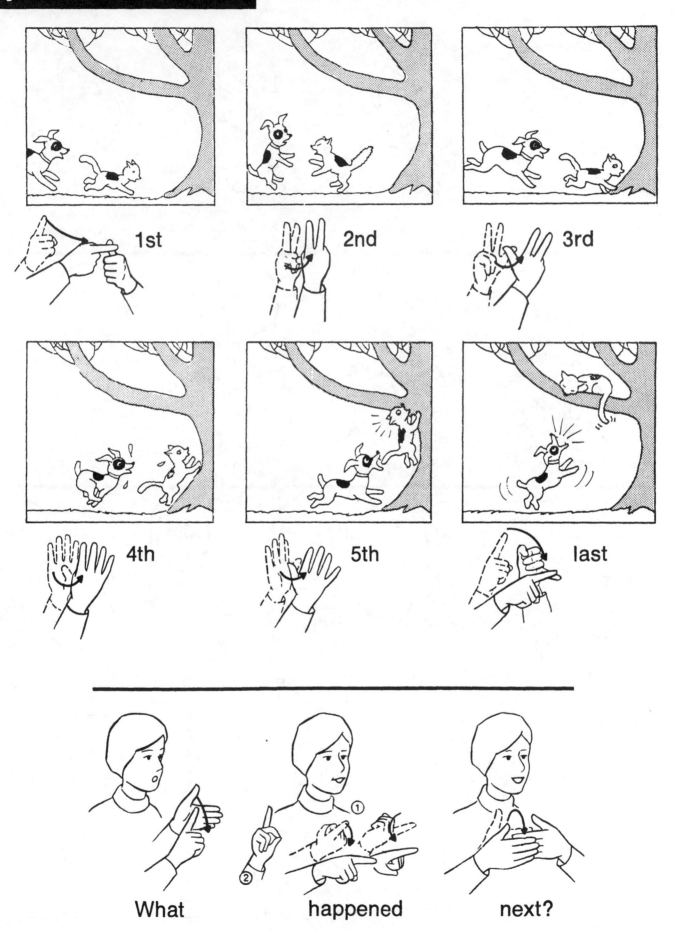

1st

2nd

3rd

4th

5th

last

What   happened   next?

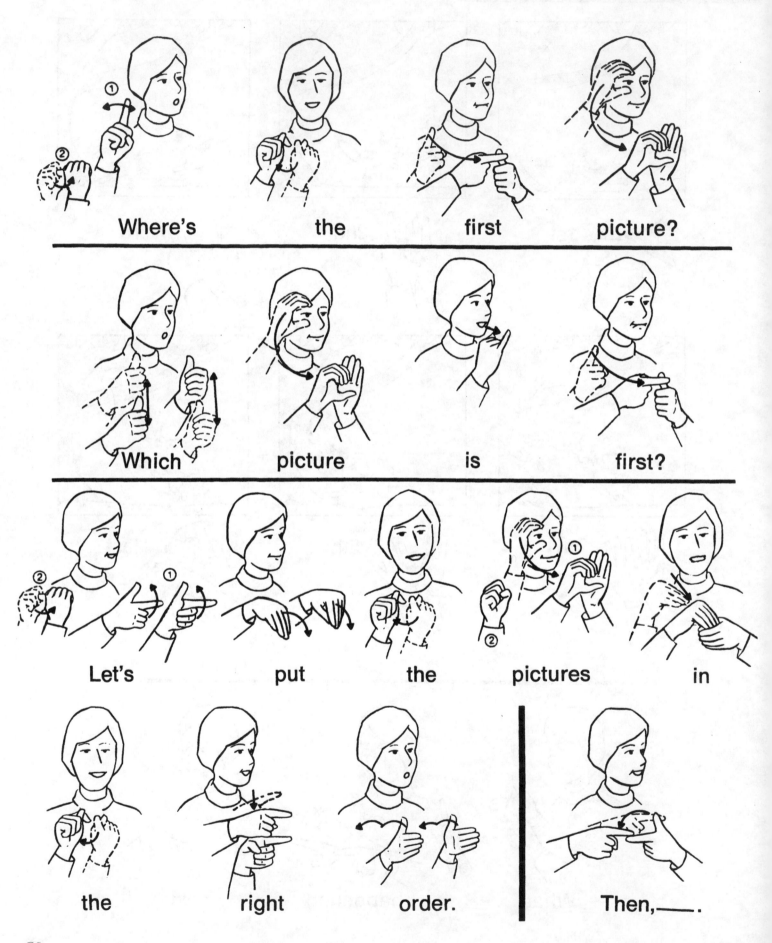

Where's the first picture?

Which picture is first?

Let's put the pictures in

the right order.

Then,_____.

Shapes and Sizes

circle

diamond

heart

rectangle

square

star

triangle

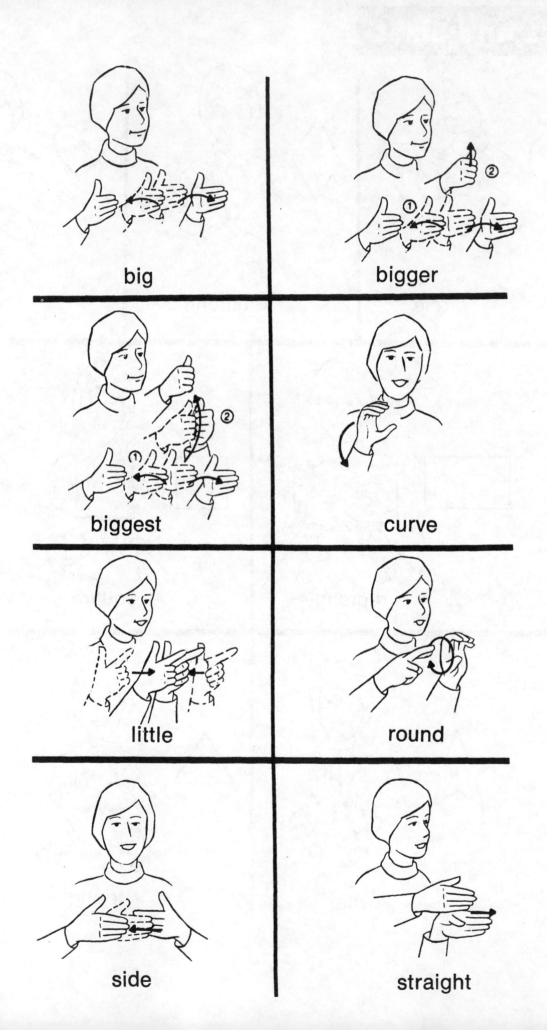

big

bigger

biggest

curve

little

round

side

straight

Copy   this   figure.   Cross   out ___.

Draw   a   circle   around ___.

Look   at   the   first   (next)   line.

Put   a   line   under ___.   Trace ___.

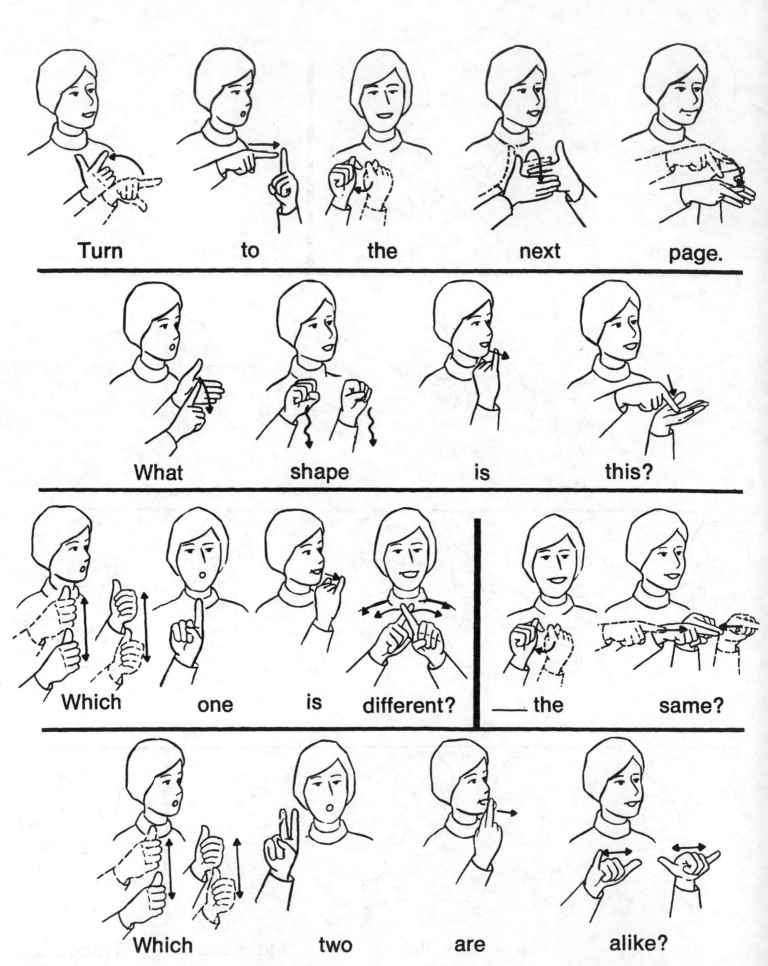

Turn   to   the   next   page.

What   shape   is   this?

Which   one   is   different?   ___ the   same?

Which   two   are   alike?

Snack Time

chocolate

coke

cookie

cracker

cup

empty

full

glass

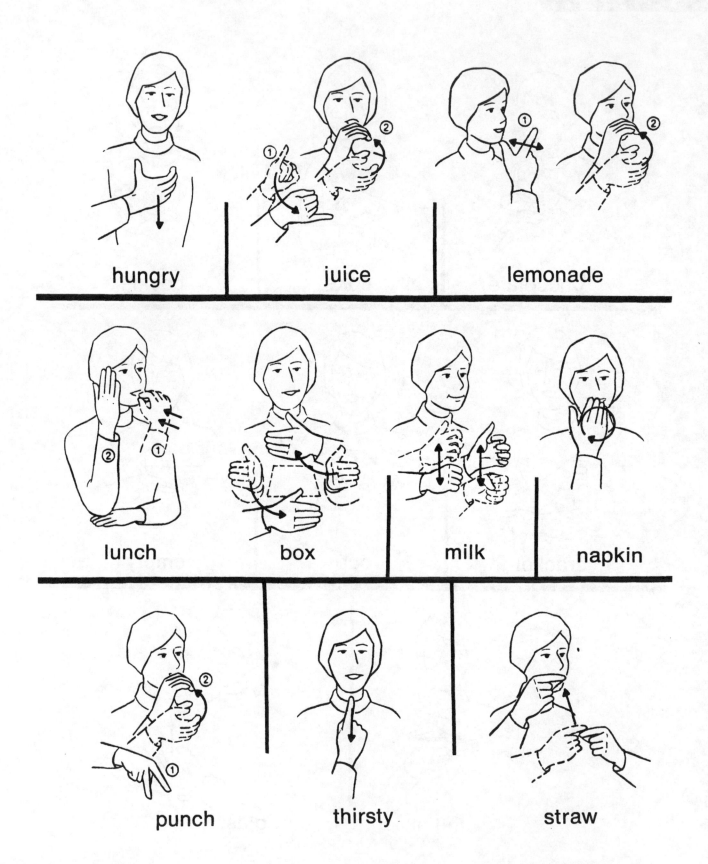

hungry juice lemonade

lunch box milk napkin

punch thirsty straw

56

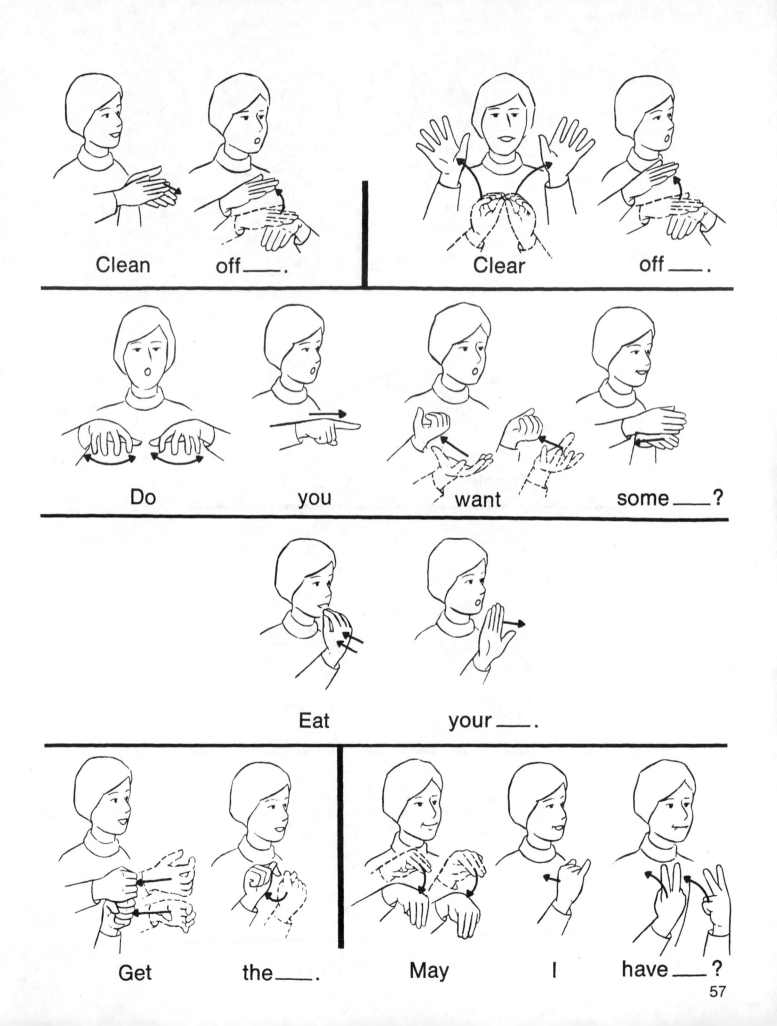

Clean off _____ . | Clear off _____ .

Do you want some _____ ?

Eat your _____ .

Get the _____ . | May I have _____ ?

57

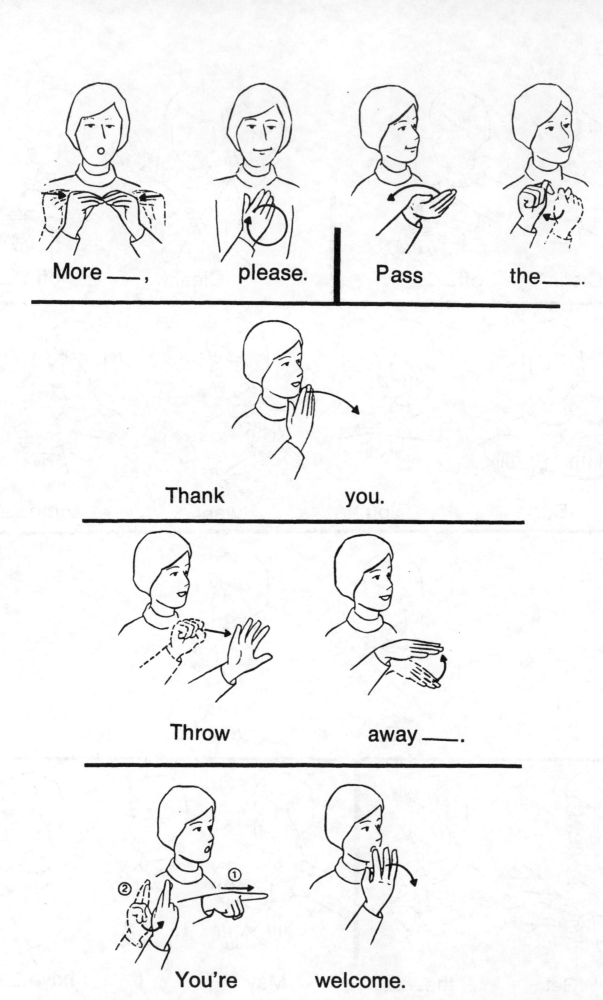

More ____ , please. | Pass the____.

Thank you.

Throw away ____.

You're welcome.

58

Speech Training

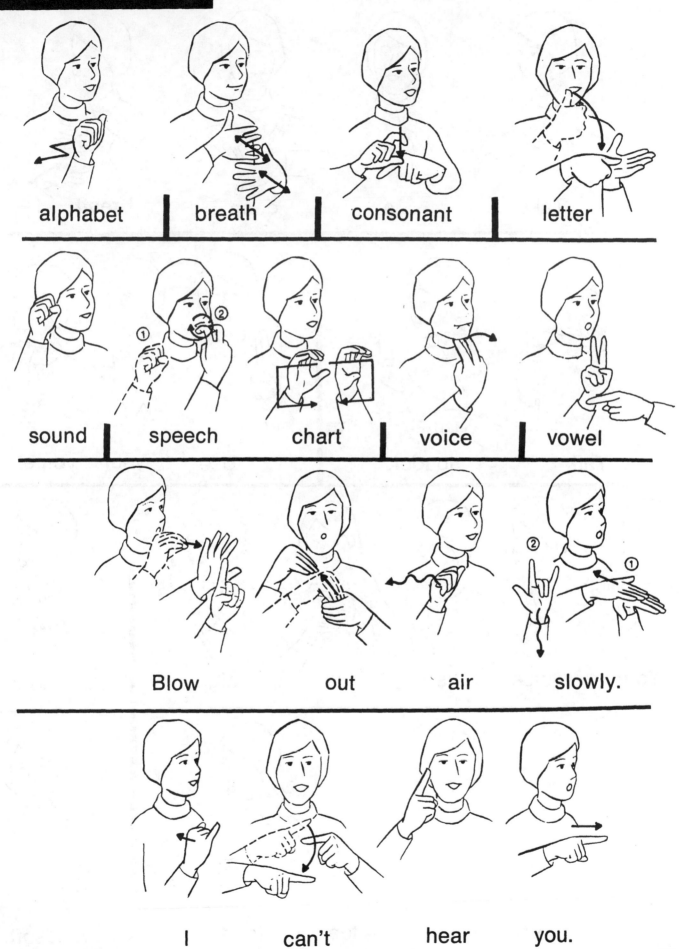

alphabet	breath	consonant	letter

sound	speech	chart	voice	vowel

Blow out air slowly.

I can't hear you.

Take   a   deep   breath.

Talk   louder.   Use   your   voice.

Your   voice   is   too   high.   ___ low.

Your   voice   is   too   loud.   ___ soft.

60

Teachers' Materials

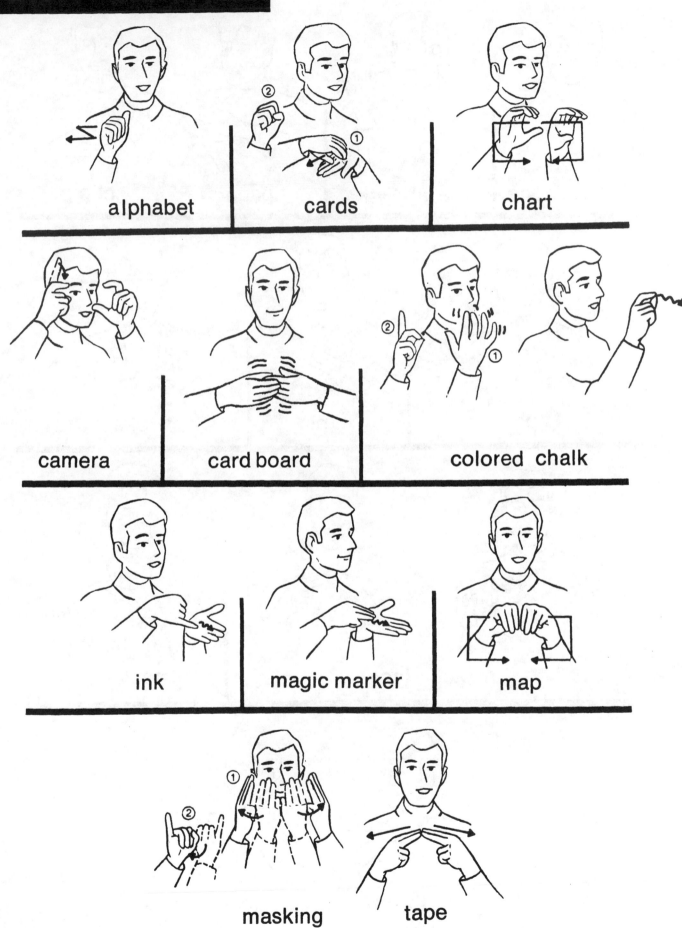

alphabet

cards

chart

camera

card board

colored chalk

ink

magic marker

map

masking

tape

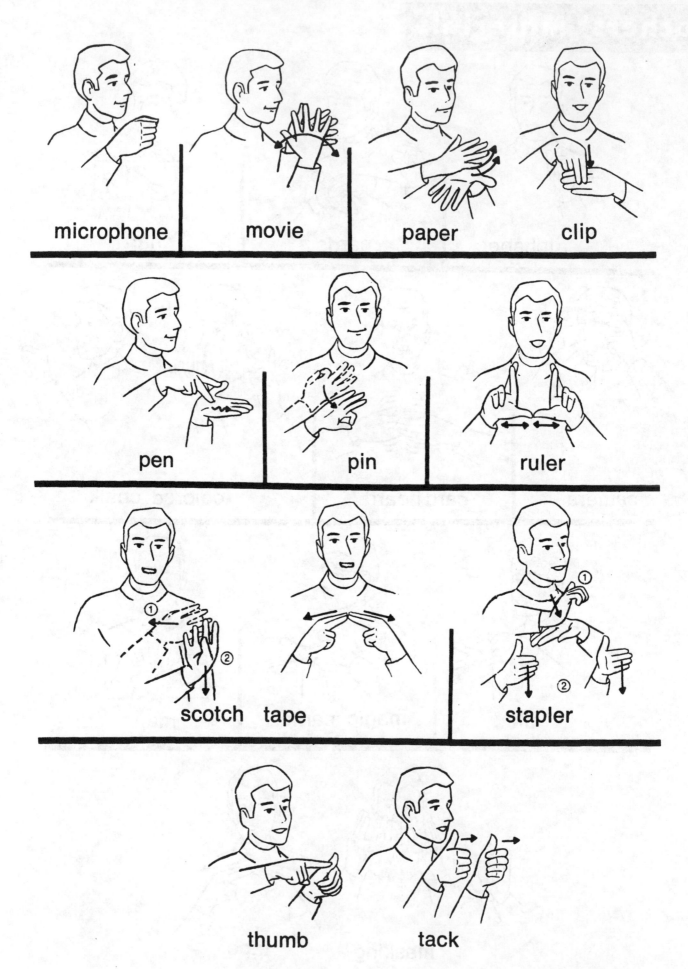

microphone   movie   paper   clip

pen   pin   ruler

scotch tape   stapler

thumb   tack

Toilet Time

clean   dirty   dry

paper   towel   sink

soap   toilet   paper

water   wet

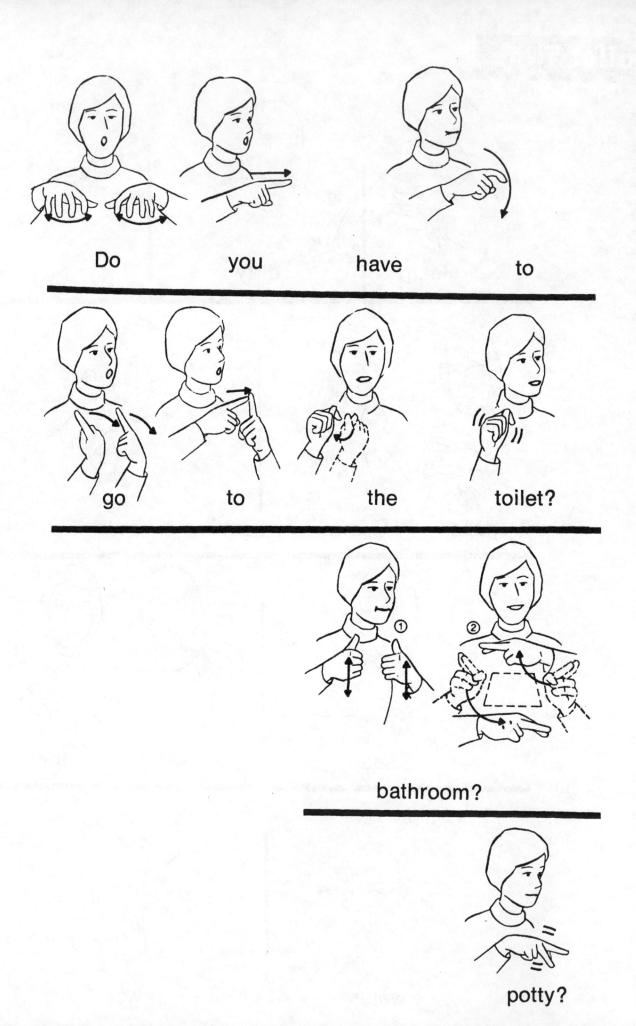

Do   you   have   to

go   to   the   toilet?

bathroom?

potty?

Flush ___ .

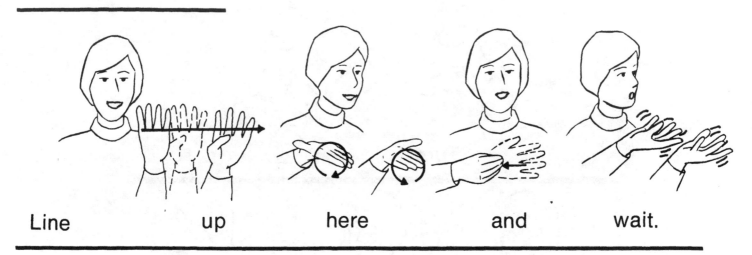

Line   up   here   and   wait.

Now   you're   nice   and   clean.

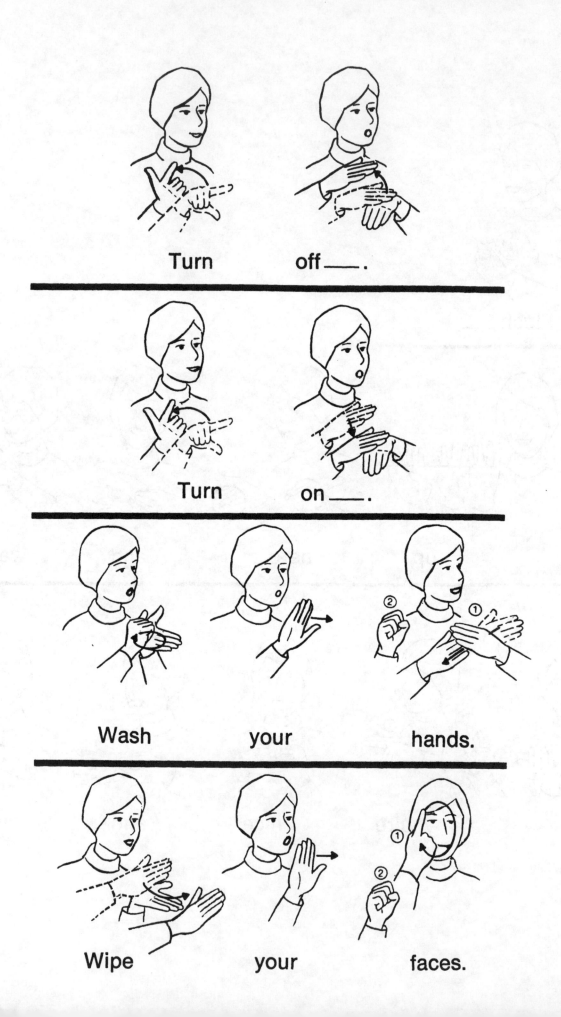

Turn   off ___ .

Turn   on ___ .

Wash   your   hands.

Wipe   your   faces.

Weather

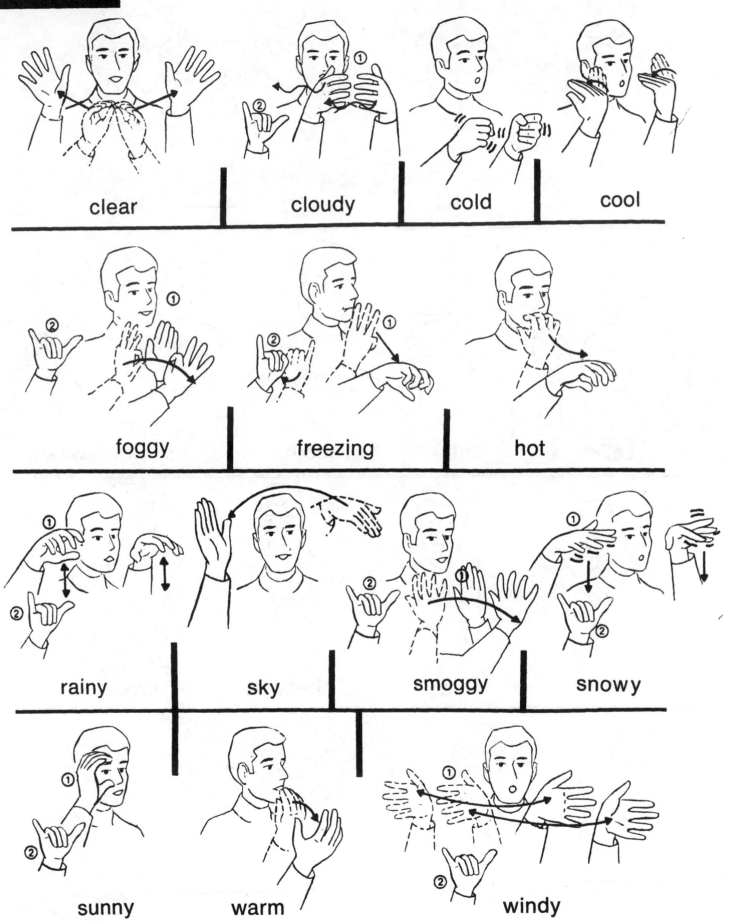

clear

cloudy

cold

cool

foggy

freezing

hot

rainy

sky

smoggy

snowy

sunny

warm

windy

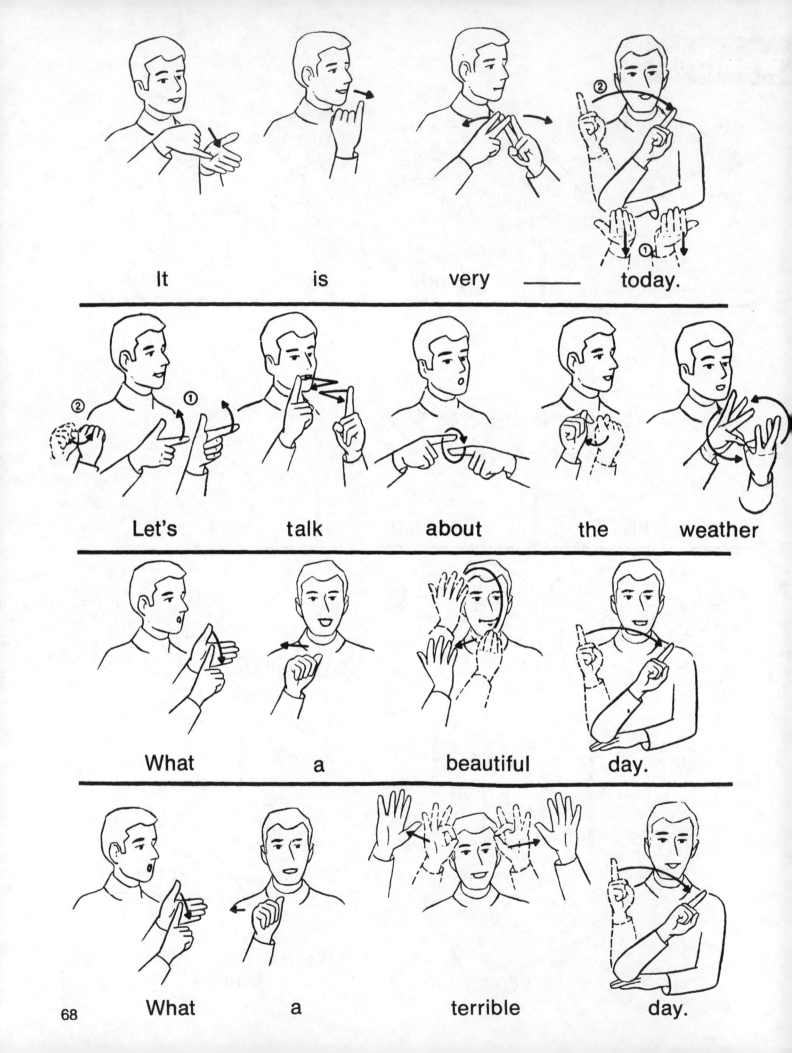

It   is   very   ——   today.

Let's   talk   about   the   weather

What   a   beautiful   day.

What   a   terrible   day.

INDEX *

PHRASES

TITLES IN THE  SERIES

The Gallaudet Signed English Project has produced books and posters designed for hearing-impaired people and others who may have problems learning English. The materials and the system logic are described in *Signed English: A Guide to Its Components and Materials.* A copy of the guide ($1.00 plus $1.00 shipping and handling) can be obtained from Gallaudet College Press, 800 Florida Avenue NE, Washington, DC 20002.

Comprehensive Reference
A complete guide to using Signed English, including 3,100 sign words and descriptions.

The Comprehensive Signed
English Dictionary

Level I: Beginning Books
Basic vocabulary, phrases, and simple sentences related to daily activities.

All by Myself
Baby's Animal Book
A Book about Me
Circus Time
Count and Color
Fire Fighter Brown
I Am a Kitten
My Toy Book
The Pet Shop
Policeman Jones
The Things I Like to Do
With My Legs

Special Purpose Books
For students who want more specialized or more basic vocabulary.

Signed English for the
Classroom
Signed English for the
Residence Hall
The Signed English Starter

Level II: Growing Up Books and Stories
High interest-level topics presented in simple, straight-forward sentences.

At Night: A First Book of
Prepositions
Cars and Trucks and Things
The Clock Book
The Gingerbread Man
Goldilocks and the Three
Bears
The Holiday Book
I Want to Be a Farmer
Little Lost Sally
Matthew's Accident
Mealtime at the Zoo
Night/Day — Work/Play
Spring Is Green
Stores
The Three Billy Goats Gruff
The Three Little Kittens
Tommy's Day
The Ugly Duckling

Signed English Posters
For classroom use or room decorations at home.

Jack and Jill
Manual Alphabet
Rock-A-Bye Baby

Level III: More Stories and Poems
Advanced language patterns. Classic fairy tales, some with complicated plots and more sophisticated vocabulary.

Be Careful
Bobby Visits the Dentist
Good Manners
Hansel and Gretel
How To
Jack and the Beanstalk
Julie Goes to School
Little Poems for Little
People
Little Red Riding Hood
Mouse's Christmas Eve
The Night before Christmas
Nursery Rhymes from
Mother Goose
Oliver in the City
Questions and More
Questions
Sand, Sea, Shells, and Sky
Songs in Signed English
(with record)
The Tale of Peter Rabbit
The Three Little Pigs
We're Going to the Doctor
When I Grow Up

The American Manual Alphabet

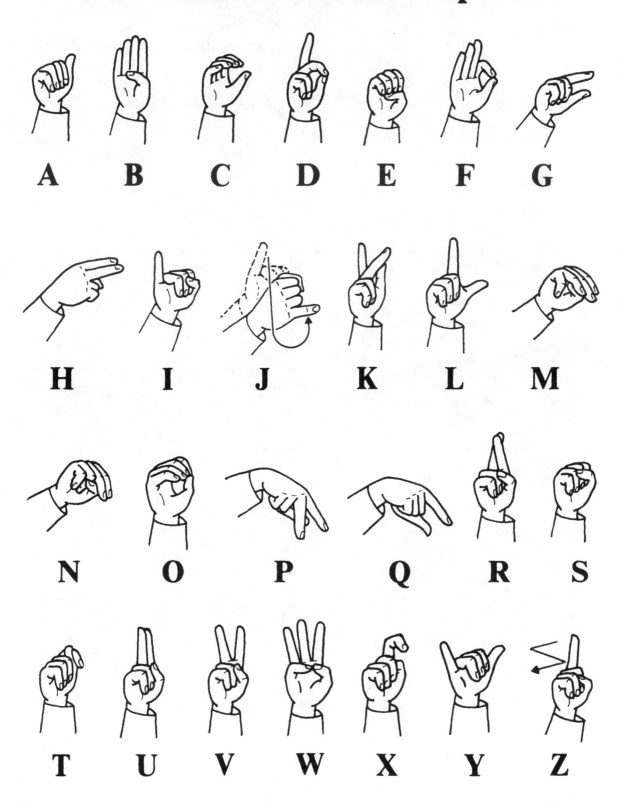

CPSIA information can be obtained
at www.ICGtesting.com
Printed in the USA
FFHW011733120219
50529906-55795FF

9 780913 580370